From Section 8 to C.E.O.
A Novel Inspired by Real-Life Events

by Kinyatta E. Gray

ALL RIGHTS RESERVED. No part of this book may be reproduced in any written, electronic, recording, or photocopying without written permission of the publisher or author. The exception would be in the case of brief quotations embodied in the critical articles or reviews and pages where permission is specifically granted by the publisher or author.

Written By: Kinyatta E. Gray © 2019
Published By: Pen Legacy®
Cover Design By: Christian Cuan
Formatting By: The Liar's Craft
Edited By: EditNow
Professional Photographs: Ksenia Pro Photography

Disclaimer: *The characters in this novel are fictional and were created for entertainment purposes only. Any character similarities are purely coincidental and are not portrayals of actual people. Portions of this novel are based on real-life events; however, significant details have been altered to avoid legal pitfalls.*

Library of Congress Cataloging – in- Publication Data has been applied for.

ISBN: 978-1-7348278-0-4
PRINTED IN THE UNITED STATES OF AMERICA.

Also by Kinyatta E. Gray

Book

30 Days: Surviving the Trauma and Unexpected Loss of a Single Parent as an Only Child (2019)

Book Anthology

Passing as Straight: Women Whose True Sexuality Went Undetected by a Judgmental Society (2020)

Dedication

This book is dedicated to single parents who are trying to raise their children while the odds seemed stacked against them, while simultaneously being courageous, determined, and driven enough to pursue their wildest dreams. **Visualize Your Success Until It Manifests**

I'm Not Here To Be Average, I'm Here To Be Awesome!
~ Unknown

Table of Contents

Prologue 1

Chapter 1..
Welcome to Heaven's World 7

Chapter 2..
This New Life Ain't Easy 28

Chapter 3..
The Climb 40

Chapter 4..
Breaking the Law at the Law Firm....................................... 56

Chapter 5..
The Biggest Sexual Harasser Ever 81

Chapter 6..
This Man Just Won't Quit... 97

Chapter 7..
The Ultimate Betrayal 102

Chapter 8..
Bruised But Not Broken 113

Chapter 9..
Hurt and Devastation 119

Chapter 10..
Another Opportunity Came Knocking................................. 132

Chapter 11..

Major Relationship Issues 144

Chapter 12..

MIA in Miami...159

Chapter 13..

I Hate Working for Women..170

Chapter 14..

Love & Stability 188

Chapter 15..

Meet My Parent 196

Chapter 16..

Moving on Up. It's Been Great, Section 8!....................................202

Chapter 17..

Climbing Higher..206

Chapter 18..

Oh No! Not Mr. Greenstein..217

Chapter 19..

Catastrophic Tragedy Rips Heaven to Pieces.................................223

Chapter 20..

Heaven Takes It ALL the Way to the Top 237

Prologue

With the umpteenth breath and the most disturbing one yet escaping her lips, Heaven cast her gaze out the window and farther away from the house she felt trapped within. Her heart yearned to be outside of those walls, her soul craved the freedom that came with not lacking, and her entire mind seconded those thoughts.

It was why she didn't hear her mother call out to her. It was why she didn't harken her attention to whatever her mom was trying to say, let alone even key into it. For Heaven, it was the same old story and warnings from Mom, warning of how wanting more (by any means necessary) might come to haunt her in the long run.

As a matter of fact, the wide-eyed teenager could not care less. She wanted more, and it felt as though it was right at her fingertips, waiting for her to make the move to get it. Granted, there were obstacles, but she was beginning to see them as ones she had to get out of sight and out of her way as soon as possible. She cleared her throat before looking down at the plate on her table. Heaven's eyes shrunk with displeasure and an obvious show of disappointment. The disappointments, born out of her desire to have more, had nothing to do with her wonderful mother. Her mom could not be faulted in any way, considering how much she had done and how well she always gave her best to make sure her daughter had a comfortable life.

Her mother had noticed but didn't care to respond as she sat in her seat opposite her daughter before plunging into her meal. Heaven's mom obviously knew what her daughter was thinking about and wasn't about to allow herself drown in thoughts over them. Yet Heaven, ambitious from an early age and with the drive and desire to get more, slowly shoved the plate her mother fixed her to the side. Doing so broke her heart, but deep within she was tired of having what she perceived to be the same meal over and over and again.

"You don't want your food?" her mother asked in a concerned tone.

"I don't have an appetite." Her lips twitched, and her fists folded into balls as she laid them on the table without uttering a single word.

"Are we going at this again tonight?" Heaven's mother slowly raised her head to look at her daughter.

Those eyes definitely bore a great deal of disappointment, and it wasn't hard to spot. It wasn't the first conversation around the dinner table, and it wasn't about to be the last. Every single one followed a single pattern, and while Heaven tried to keep her cool, it was obvious her mother was on the verge of losing hers. In a black family—or a black household, for that matter—rejecting a meal provided for and made by one's mother was a recipe for death on its own, even more so if someone is sitting opposite their mom who painstakingly made the meal. Granted, Heaven had never gone against her mother or shown her any form of disrespect. She simply wanted more, wanted something different and something better.

"We are really going to have this again tonight, aren't we?" her mother asked again.

Heaven sighed, leaned back into her chair and began to independently tap her fingers into the table. "I just cannot figure out why you wouldn't allow us do what is needed to get what we want. I know you work hard and you have been the best there is raising me by yourself, but we need more, Mama."

Her mother fell silent and resumed her meal. Heaven's mother toyed around the meal with her fork, obviously distracted and unhappy, while her daughter continued to yap like a spoiled teenager. "You could easily have gone out with Mr. Bryan and gotten more than enough from him to prevent us from eating the same meals every single night!" Heaven stated dramatically. "Don't you want better?" Her mother shoved her plate away and responded, "Better never comes from shortcuts! It never comes from having to bypass the normal ways to success, and it sure as hell wouldn't ever give you what you want in the long run!

And, baby, don't you ever depend on a man for your success in life. If you remember nothing else after I am gone, remember to thrive, be a fighter, an independent woman and spirit who can make it with or without a man."

Heaven scoffed, but not derisively to insult her mother, shook her head, and continued to shake her head at the notion behind her mother's reasoning. She had seen families, and parents most especially; doing things she was sure her morally upright mother wouldn't in any way dally into for whatever reasons. "Look outside the window, Mom! Other families are enjoying better lives even with their mother being single parents!" Heaven said. "You know what I think?"

Her mother ignored the question, knowing full well her daughter was about to tell her, regardless. "You are just too scared to do what would get us out of this situation we've been living in for a while now. I so cannot wait to have my freedom, and this isn't because I don't appreciate everything you have done, but I believe we can get more, Mama, and I want much more." Heaven knew precisely what she was trying to pass across as a message to her mother, whom she believed was too upright in life to go for what she wanted, or to even attempt to break the rules to secure more gains.

"What would you have me do? Find ways to act like most women would? Do you understand how far or how dangerous this precedence can become for you?" her mother asked in a tone and with a smirk. Responding in a slightly elevated tone, Heaven replied, "Anything is possible. I would do anything possible to succeed, and I don't care if I have to cut corners or even skip due processes to get what I need." She was done playing fair as her mother had always done. She never saw how fairness or playing by the rules benefitted her mom. But nevertheless, Heaven respected her mom and admired her resolve and determination. Heaven sought what others had, and she wanted the good life, too, wherever it might be and however she might get it.

"You foolish girl." Her mother sighed. "You are going to get yourself in a hell of a mess."

Heaven had heard enough from her mom, and she removed herself from the seat. She eyed the meal she had been served and fantasized about what wealthy families or those willing to compromise their values, which her mother wouldn't, were having for the night.

"Getting messy at times is the only way to get what you need in this life, Mother. I love you dearly, Mommy, but I just cannot change who I am." She turned away and headed out the door and into the night with the intent to be different, she couldn't fathom being what her mother wanted her to be, by doing things the "right" way. Heaven couldn't do things the right way, she had to be daring. "Whatever it takes" was the anthem she sang as she disappeared into the night.

For Heaven, she would do whatever it takes to get her life into the form she wished for and that she admired others for. It didn't matter what she had to do and what corners she would have to cut. She dipped her hand into her jeans pocket, dialed her partner-in-crime's digits, and raised the phone to her ear as it connected within seconds. "Hey, girl! Are you still down for going to Houston's in exchange for some crazy fun tonight?" She smiled as she heard her best friend agree without asking further questions. It was what Heaven loved about Michell—they were cut from similar cloths. They would both cut corners through life if and when they felt it was necessary.

"Damn the consequences," she muttered to herself before disappearing into the night.

Chapter 1

Welcome to Heaven's World

Beads of sweat trickled down her cheeks as she clamped her eyelids shut for the umpteenth time. Everything about the air felt bothersome, and being where she was did nothing to assist her anxiety. Yet there was no leaving, or at least she couldn't dare attempt to do so.

Copious amount of thoughts trickled through her mind, and each came with profound negativity. A little bit positivity or enthusiasm would certainly go a long way in calming her nerves, but the harder she tried, the harder it became. It only caused her to exude more sweat, jitter where she sat, and adjust herself uncomfortably every few seconds on her seat.

Her lips trembled but barely let off a single word other than exhaustive sigh. If there was one test she was being put through, she would guess it was one of patience, and she was beginning to get to the point of not caring anymore.

Hours had passed, or maybe minutes, but it definitely felt like hours. Time continued to trickle by and cast her mind toward unnecessary thoughts and emotions.

"Heaven Glory Davis! You are next!" a voice announced and dragged Heaven out from her deep and baffling thoughts.

Quite frankly, she had been caught off guard, and there was no hiding it by the manner in which she jumped up to look around. She let off a loud gasp in shock and to show her appreciation as words failed her in that moment. She had just been informed that her wait was almost over, and not just that, but that her name had made it over to the top of the wait list for Section 8. Her emotions threatened to run wild, and her eyes darted around the room endlessly. Her previously clenched fists slowly eased into a more relaxed position, but it didn't last long before she felt the same stings of nervousness and anxiety riddle down her spine once again. It felt worse now; she was closer to her goal and there was no telling how things would turn out. The anxiety only worsened as she leaned back into her seat and thought about how the journey began and the amount of time the entire ordeal had taken from her.

"Finally," she whispered to herself before sighing aloud again and not for the last time.

For Heaven, the wait had taken five long years, and it didn't seem like it would come to an end. In DC, the mandatory waiting period for anyone with a family of two on the Section 8 wait list was three to five solid years without any form of compromise. The journey had initially felt like an impossible one, and even Heaven never trusted she was going to make it through those five years without becoming absolutely overwhelmed by everything around her. It was why the night before was the longest one she had ever experienced in her life. Restlessness, anxiety, and some degree of depression had slowly crept in. She paced along the floor, glancing at her documents in her hands, checking and rechecking them over and over and again to be sure she was right and that nothing was out of place. Through all these periods of anxiety, her heart threatened to implode, her circulation ran wildly with copious amount of blood being pumped by the raging heart, and her knees wobbled and threatened to fail her once or twice. For Heaven, everything had to be in order; it had taken five painstaking years, and she just could not accept anything less.

While Heaven sat, she lowered her head and closed her eyes again as she muttered quietly, "Five years." She had counted every single day, marked it on the calendar to be sure she wasn't about to miscount the entire process, and equally tasked herself with subtracting what she had left in days until this very moment. The ordeal was mind numbing, mentally challenging, and at times, emotionally drowning to think about, but it was her burden to bear and she had done just that.

Getting as far as she had in the tiresome process, Heaven wasn't about to grant anything the opportunity to fuck things up for her. With the thought in mind, she unzipped her bag, took out her documents, and began to peruse the contents once again. She didn't care if she had gone through them a thousand times already. "One more time… Just one more look," she recited to herself absentmindedly.

Considering the circumstances surrounding her life over the past five years, for Heaven, this was the only solution in sight. Being where she was would be penance for every single distress she had undergone over the years. It wasn't much, but it was more than enough or would be more than enough. It was how she felt and it was exactly what she had etched to mind from the beginning. Ever since the birth of her first child, her little darling girl, Hillary Clinton Davis-Buffett, Heaven had been living with her mom on an on-and-off basis. Heaven had named her daughter after the presidential candidate Hillary Rodham Clinton, noting the importance of at least bestowing the child with an influencing, powerful and well-respected name, regardless of the fact she was born into a pretty modest home with an equally modest background. They nicknamed her "Hilly from Philly," which was a nod to one of Heaven's favorite singers, Jill Scott, who is from Philadelphia. Heaven shuffled between her mother's house and living with Hilly's dad, Bradley Buffett, also known as Breezy Buff, who was practically living in a friend's basement. It wasn't the best choice, but it was all Heaven had and what she could work with.

Heaven and Breezy's tale began when they first met

in high school, after he had just been crowned winner of DC Rap Stars Talent Show. Everything about him had tickled her fancy and almost caused her to lose her breath, but one thing stood above everything else—he was white. As of that moment, this was a serious and immediate turn-on for Heaven, which blinded her from most or all other shortcomings. Being in his presence would take her breath away and sweep her off of her feet without a moment's notice.

Breezy had been one of those affluent white boys who made an extra effort to be exactly what their parents didn't want them to be. His ways contradicted his parents' wishes in every way, and he never seemed to worry about the repercussions of being who he was. In fact, it was safe to say Breezy was a poster boy for what white kids did culturally wrong.

Breezy was a well-known rapper who also had a penchant for never being able to keep his dick away from every single black woman who came his way. It is safe to say Breezy was what most girls in high school, who wanted nothing more than to become renegades, dearly craved for or wanted. Heaven made it her mission to find out why most girls wanted the obvious bad boy.

Upon winning the DC Rap Stars Talent Show, Breezy had gotten himself into trouble not long afterward; he almost got beat up by the previous year's winner and his friends. It had been a terrible humiliation that a white boy won over a black guy, who presumably felt rapping was a spot reserved for blacks. Quite fairly, though, the dude might have taken home the crown once again had he not punched one of the judges a few years back. The cash prize was $500 and a plaque bearing Breezy's name on it, which was later placed in the Sunset High School Hall of Fame. This win absolutely secured Breezy's popularity among students and like-minded people around the school. It had also gone a step further in cementing the possibility of getting down with Heaven, if she could actually manage to get his attention. Heaven was secretly bisexual, but never passed up a great opportunity that came her way, regardless of gender.

After Breezy won the talent show, more than enough thirsty females came out from everywhere, competing for his mystical dick. The after-party to commemorate the celebration of the event's success was slated to happen at the local IHOP.

Heaven and her friend Michell headed over to the restaurant immediately after the talent show to meet an overwhelming crowd, packed full and with little to no space to breathe freely.

Breezy definitely seemed to be enjoying his victory, high-fiving and dapping up all of his "fans." His number of followers more than doubled after his win, and they weren't just local or those he attended school with. Breezy had done well enough to win several rap battles in other high schools for him to become well recognized and respected throughout the county. His past wins were countless, and the future, without doubt, looked bright. The moment Heaven and her friend walked into the restaurant, they scanned around carefully, searching for who might turn out to be Heaven's biggest competitor to prevent her from getting on Breezy's radar. One person stood out among every other girl in there.

With a smirk on Heaven's face and a rather cynical one being mirrored by Michell, both ladies devised a plan for that chic named Sonja. She was well known by the nickname "Sexy Sonja" in school, and quite frankly, she was a cross between Beyoncé and Ciara. She was hot, no doubt, and a slender frame of threat to everything Heaven had in mind. There were elements about Sonja that baffled people—like if her hair was a weave or real. She got her hair done at Kloe Hair Designers in Hyattsville, Maryland, a high-end salon where everyone goes for undetectable weaves. Everything about her was undeniably on point, and there was never a time you could catch her off her game. Her slender, long body with a cute, curved butt was just enough to fit perfectly into Seven For All Mankind jeans. There was no enigma as to why she was so appealing, not to mention how ridiculously smart she was. There was the added advantage that she lived in the uppity black neighborhoods and her father was a Fox-5 DC news correspondent.

Michell stepped outside and headed for the IHOP parking lot where she spotted Sonja's 3 series BMW. Heaven knew exactly whom she needed when she was in the mood for devious acts, and Michell was all about that life.

Michell had previously armed herself with the pink bat from Heaven's trunk, smirking and smiling devilishly as she approached the BMW. Swinging as hard as her arms would permit her, she struck hard at Sonja's window, setting off her car alarm immediately and shattering the window. Hurriedly, Michell disappeared from the crime scene, back to Heaven's car to hide the weapon, before making her way back to IHOP as though she had done nothing wrong. Not much longer, almost immediately after Michell had returned, everyone's attention was dragged to the siren's blaring sound. Eyes gazed out of the windows in curiosity before someone in the crowd shouted, "Shit! Sonja! That's your fucking car!"

Sonja took off her heels, neglecting how gorgeous she looked, to attend to her wailing car immediately. It would be the last time Heaven had to worry about Sonja or see her for the rest of the night. It was a beautifully worked plan and a perfectly executed one as well. It gave Michell and Heaven the opportunity to meet in the restaurant's bathroom as the commotion ensued to exchange hearty and devilish high-fives. "Next phase of the plan," Heaven muttered as she winked to her dear friend. She walked toward the mirror in the bathroom, pulled out her MAC lip-gloss and slicked her edges down a little more before making sure everything about her body was tight and right. Taking extra precautions, Heaven finally felt satisfied enough to head out of the bathroom and toward Breezy's table without attempting any detour or distractions along the way.

"Excuse me! Excuse me! Excuse me!" Heaven muttered every single time as she walked through the maze of bodies in a bid to get to Breezy. Making it over to him wasn't easy, but she did it. He had just finished eating a meat lover's omelet and was waiting on his iced tea refill when she arrived at his table. Her timing was just perfect, ironically so too, since Breezy had specifically demanded he wanted peace and quiet and to be alone before his food arrived. He looked up at her immediately, noticing her presence with a sparkle in his eyes. "What's up, shawty?" Heaven found herself mesmerized to hear how urban he sounded even when he wasn't rapping. *Now, that's a serious turn-on*, she thought. He motioned for her to come closer, and Heaven did, boldly and with a wild smile across her face. "Nothing much," she replied. "What's good with you?" Breezy shrugged. "Well, here I am trying to find out what's good with your sexy self."

He was slick, no doubt, and it only enticed Heaven more, without an ounce of guilt riding in her heart over getting Sonja's car fucked up and automatically out of her way. She felt vindicated and happy with the fact that she was just about to find out more about "Big" Breezy. Heaven smiled at him and leaned closer into his table so he could perceive the generous and alluring scent from her Lolita Lempicka perfume. Her weave shone brilliantly, while she did her best to show off the quality it was made of and the difference from those worn by those basic bitches. "My mom is in South Africa all week. The house is mine, and I am definitely in the mood to get to know you better," she said with a wink.

Breezy smiled back, obviously picking up the vibes and willing to go along with it. He leaned in as well, making sure his warm breath could be felt by Heaven as his eyes locked in gaze with hers.

"It all depends," he whispered. Heaven slowly raised her right brow, waiting for what he had to say. "I don't fuck with nobody that don't know how to give head." It was an invitation with a test laid out straight. She smirked and smacked her lips seductively while the two stared at each other for a while. He was definitely flirty, just the way she wanted him to be and the way she liked her men to be. Being rigid was never a standard, and it was a serious turn-off as well. "It is good, because I give the best," she replied cockily. Breezy cocked his head, leaned backward, and said, "Check, please!"

This was how things had begun, and the beginning of a long-term relationship between Breezy and Heaven. They barely had five months to kill before graduation, and they decided to spend an enormous amount of time together. It was a perfect example of how spending one night together turns into pure love from the first night together. It definitely wasn't what Breezy had planned, and it wasn't what Heaven had assumed would happen, either. It was a happy occurrence born from an unexpected situation.

Oddly enough, the notion that she would pass to be with him only if she could give head turned out to be nothing but shit-talk after they left the restaurant together. In fact, there was no fucking—in one of the most bizarre turn of events for Heaven, who definitely had her mind fixated on a whole lot of naughtiness ensuing. Instead, the duo sat in Breezy's car, close to the Reagan National Airport, watching the airplanes land, laughing at one another's corny jokes and making plans about the future. It was absolutely the best night Heaven had spent with a guy out of the blue, and one that was bound to remain ingrained in her mind forever.

For the next few months, things would roll over smoothly and wonderfully. Heaven found some form of safe haven in Breezy, and being his girl was nothing but pride for her. It felt even sweeter and more perfect considering the multitudes of girls Breezy could have chosen from.

In May 1997, just one month shy of graduation, the big news struck Heaven like a bad and an unexpected blow. She found out she was six-weeks pregnant, carrying white boy Breezy's baby. The knowledge was drowning and equally confusing. The world seemed to stop moving, and the earth beneath her felt overwhelming to even exist on.

Heaven needed help, and she sought her mother out immediately. This woman was the first and sole person Heaven could or would speak to about the revelation. The level of closeness and bond she shared with her mother had also been a determining and helpful factor; they shared and talked about everything without ever hiding any secrets from one another. Surprisingly, her mother accepted the pregnancy without castigation or any guilt tripping. She understood Heaven's plight because she was once in her daughter's shoes; she had had Heaven as a young lady and with no choice but to raise the girl on her own after Heaven's father tragically passed away in a plane crash while on business, before Heaven was born.

    Everything she knew about him had come from the memories her mom shared freely over the years. Once her mother was on board and willing to support her unexpected pregnancy, Heaven sought to break the news to Breezy. It took her a while to contemplate telling him, but there was no choice but to do so.

    Breezy had a tender side to him, which Heaven had learned over the past few months they had been together. Tears rushed down his face after she told him, and he cried in joyous tone about the unexpected pregnancy. His precise words had been, "I want a beautiful princess with my black queen."

    The following month, Heaven would graduate from high school, with the feeling of love engulfing her more than she had ever felt.

    Soon after Heaven had informed her mother of her pregnancy, her mom had advised her to head over to DC Housing Authority to submit an application for housing. Her mom knew too well the baby was going to be a challenge and create some setbacks, regardless of what Heaven might think. There was bound to be some moments of struggle for Heaven, and there would be moments of relief for her with housing to help alleviate some of her financial burdens. Heaven's mother fervently warned her daughter to consider the support as a bridge toward attaining something better, and also to keep herself grounded and not become complacent relying on government support. The support was meant to become a means of transition as she developed a strategy for the future.

Who their right frame of mind who would want the government in their life permanently, constantly dictating and depicting who can live with them in their home, as well as whether they could paint the walls in their own home? Heaven got a good understanding of how housing programs worked and knew all too well that it was bound to take some years before any housing assistance would come through. Following her mother's desires, she applied for the support sooner than later and decided she'd weather the storm until things clicked into place.

After graduating from high school and while pregnant, Heaven immediately found a job working at Costco as a cashier. The work was tiresome and challenging, but the money was needed, especially for the incoming baby. Her previous plans to go to college for Radiology wound up becoming delayed for the future. Breezy, on the other hand, has a great uncle, the billionaire Wadley Buffett. He's a real estate tycoon, far bigger than Donald Trump, and the entire Buffett clan worked for him in the Buffett Real Estate Firm, including Breezy's parents. His family was wealthy and hugely despised the fact that Breezy identified as "trans-black." This only transformed into Breezy being treated like the runt of the litter and getting less than he was entitled to or to what someone in his shoes and background would be given.

In fact, Breezy was given a meager stipend that was stipulated to be cut off once he graduated high school. They had also laid down an ultimatum to him: cut Heaven and her baby off, or be totally disowned by the family. Breezy, proud in his own right, loving Heaven and his unborn child, chose the latter and immediately found himself drowning in the same financial circle as Heaven, being just above broke.

Heaven felt pleased and was in absolute admiration for a man who was willing to accept and choose her over his family's threat about being disowned and cut off. She felt immeasurable pride that Breezy picked her and their baby over money, but resented the simple fact that neither she nor her baby would be entitled to the Buffett family wealth, all because they were black. Indifferent to how things had panned out, Heaven had figured her life would attain some stability and financial backing when she first fell in love with Breezy, just before his family decided to make things hell for him. It felt like a plan washed down the drain and an ultimate failure.

Regardless, Heaven's mother had done everything in her power to prepare her daughter for circumstances turning around on her in an unpleasant manner. She had raised Heaven to be a strong, independent, and self-sufficient woman.

It helped buffer the effect of circumstances as soon as she found out that she was pregnant. In fact, Heaven plunged into taking steps to ensure she could attain some measure of stability for her baby and herself, regardless of what input or how things imparted Breezy and the relationship they had together.

Seven months later, Heaven gave birth to a beautiful, bouncing baby girl. The gorgeous baby girl resembled one created on special order from God. Her skin shone beautifully, rich in melanin features like that of her mother, with the added beauty of subtle traces of Caucasian features from her father. She had brown hair, thick and curly and fat cheeks with two deep dimples.

From the moment Breezy set his eyes on her, he was nothing but smitten and found himself falling in love with his black queen and princess all over again. It was safe to say everything felt perfect and it seemed like nothing could ever go wrong. Well, it felt perfect until Heaven received an unexpected visitor.

During Heaven's stay in the hospital, she received an unexpected visitor within the early hours of three in the morning. Breezy's mom. The woman had arrived by private car in the moment her son wasn't around; Breezy had just left to get some rest; he'd return the following morning to get Heaven and the baby. Was it a bit of coincidence, or proper planning? Heaven didn't know. Heaven parted her eyes after feeling the presence of another in her room. She awakened to the frightening sight of Breezy's mother standing over her. She glared down at Heaven, causing the new mother to worry and fear for her life. Heaven glanced toward her daughter to ascertain her safety, before looking back at the terrifying woman by her bed.

"How much is it going to take?" the woman said bluntly with a stern expression on her face.

Heaven struggled for words, groggy from the procedures of childbirth, and replied, "Two days."

Breezy's mother shook her head fervently. "No. I am asking about how much it will take for you and this little baby to disappear forever."

Heaven gained proper consciousness now and slowly dragged herself into a sitting position. Slowly, she reached for the call button by the side of her bed, hoping a nurse would arrive soon, before going the extra mile of searching for her cell phone.

"Time is of the essence for me," Breezy's mother said. "How much is it going to be?"

Heaven secretly toggled through her phone and set the voice recorder into action. It was the best she could do if she was going to get Breezy to believe her. It sounded absurd just on the face of it, but it broke Heaven's heart as well. Feigning some degree of ignorance, Heaven cleared her throat and replied, "Sorry, but I didn't quite hear you."

Breezy's mother replied in a staunch tone. "I am asking you how much it will take to have you and this baby disappear forever from our lives and from that of our son." Heaven slowly got herself into a better sitting position, breasts dripping with milk and sanitary pad moving out of place as she shot Breezy's mother a staunch stare. "Who the fuck do you think you are?" The woman seemed undaunted and continued to glare at Heaven, calmly, but with an air of worry too.

"Bitch, I will mop your white ass up and down the maternity ward if you ever come up here disrespecting me, my man, or my baby ever again!" Heaven threatened.

Her words definitely didn't pack a punch, judging by the awkward smile on Breezy mother's face. "We are not for sale, you crazy, old ass bitch!" Heaven said. "By the way, let it eat you up on the inside that my black baby girl is now a Buffett too." Heaven smirked with a sense of satisfaction. Heaven's smile didn't last long, as she didn't see what was coming. Mrs. Buffett stepped closer, swiped her hand fast enough to smack the living hell out of Heaven just as the nurse walked into the room. She had raised her hand up once again, hoping to follow up her previous action with a more daunting slap before the nurse raced to Heaven's aid and held Mrs. Buffett's hand back.

"Can someone please call the police!" the nurse cried for help. "Security! Security! Can someone please get the security?" Heaven definitely wasn't letting such an act slide off without a response. Still in pain from childbirth, she held her stomach firmly with her left hand, before leaning forward to grab hold of Mrs. Buffett's hair. Heaven yanked and dragged as aggressively as she could until she had Mrs. Buffett falling face-flat into her sweaty bed sheets. The nurse's screams echoed and traveled past the room, seeing she was no match for Heaven or able to control the mayhem that was ensuing.

Heaven continued her assault on the woman, ensuring she wasn't ever going to be disrespected in such manner ever again. Heaven beat that ass.

"Don't you fucking ever touch me again, you bitch! You rotten bitch!" Heaven yanked at the woman's hair, hearing her scream for mercy and attempt to fight her way out of it to no avail. Security soon arrived, rushing into the room. They were accompanied by police officers as well, and within minutes they carted Mrs. Buffett away, arresting her for assault. Heaven ground her teeth, fumed, and could barely control her breath as she glared at the woman being forcefully taken away.

She checked on the safety of her baby and reached for

her phone to call Breezy immediately to explain what had occurred. She wanted her man to know how his mother had assaulted her, with proof, before she fought back.

"Just hold on, babe. I will be right there," Breezy assured her. He kept true to his word and arrived within an hour of her call. Looking drained and obviously lacking sleep, Breezy walked into the room and hugged Heaven immediately. He planted warm kisses on her neck before going to look at the baby and ensured she was all right too.

"Where is she?" Breezy asked in an angry tone but not a loud one. He wasn't one to get angry easily, and Heaven could count the number of times she had seen him become even cross. Heaven explained that the police had taken his mother into custody. The nurses returned to the room to clean up Heaven. The baby cried aloud, prompting one of the nurses to hand her over to Heaven, who gazed into the eyes of her little gem, ready to nurse baby Hillary Clinton Davis-Buffett.

Humiliated by the occurrence, degraded and defamed in every possible way she could think, Heaven saw a side to the Buffett family she had never seen. She saw that white rich people could be ghetto as fuck. The woman had obviously gotten the approval of others to come over to make such an audacious request. It was easy to spot the dislike and the need to do away with Heaven and her child in Mrs. Buffett's eyes. The deed itself was incomprehensible, and the manner in which she had asked Heaven to accept her offer was demeaning. It brought the new mother hurt and caused her racial discomfort too. It wasn't the nicest way to go about things, and the Buffetts, with the exception of Breezy, obviously had their ideologies, and they could not be changed.

"How can anyone not want you?" Heaven had asked herself while she breastfed her baby girl. Her eyes were pure and innocent, her smile and the manner in which she wriggled was cute to watch and a joy to experience. The incident was nothing short of disheartening, and Heaven never wanted to experience such again. She also came to realize she had been looking at things, or at least the Buffetts, wrong.

"I want nothing to do with them ever again," she declared to herself with hot tears rolling down her cheeks. "I want nothing to do with the Buffett family." It was the best decision she felt she could make, considering the level of insult levied against her.

"I will do everything within my powers to provide for you," Heaven promised her child on that day with tear-soaked eyes and trembling lips. She made the promise to accomplish her desires, with or without Breezy or anyone else. It was the best she could do for her daughter, after all.

"I still can't believe she would do this." Breezy lamented and dragged Heaven's focus back to the room. She wasn't sure if he had heard her making the bold promise to their daughter, but she didn't care. He looked unsettled and obviously befuddled about the claims Heaven had made. Heaven scrolled through her phone, played the recording for him to listen to, and watched his face suddenly grow red with rage. He looked at her with tear-filled eyes, looked back at the phone as though he could literally see the hurtful words tearing into Heaven and then back at her again. The realization that his mother was such a sad being caused Breezy distress as he raked his fingers through his hair in a show of anxiety and disbelief.

"I am sorry," Breezy said. "I am so sorry." Heaven managed a weak smile as she pulled him closer to her bed. "I will never have anything to do with them ever again," he promised.

Heaven trusted his words but felt it didn't actually matter anymore. The worst had been done, and she was ready to stick to her guns and never allow her daughter undergo such level of humiliation ever again.

By morning, baby Hillary Clinton Davis-Buffett and Heaven were released from the hospital in perfect condition to begin their lives together as a family. It was the best feeling Heaven had ever felt in her life and one she was bound to remember till her last living breath.

Chapter 2

This New Life Ain't Easy

Time trickled past, and the experience of motherhood came with mix of emotions and experiences for Heaven. Hillary grew really fast, adored her father, and got the same measure of love, if not more, in return. Everything seemed perfect, but things weren't good financially, and the struggles were becoming overwhelming. Being cut off from his parents was a toll even Breezy had not expected to be much on him, and every single day only felt more terrible than the last.

Being who he was, his upbringing and the level of privilege he had enjoyed growing up, the ability to hold down a job for so long—and a menial paying one, for that matter—was a daunting task for Breezy. Abiding by the same rules, which the rest who obviously understood the reality of what a harsh life was, remained an impossible task for Breezy.

His longest stay on a job was two weeks before he'd get himself fired for one misdemeanor or the other, and when he walked through the door, Heaven could tell he had been laid-off yet again. "They can go fuck themselves! I don't need this shit!" Breezy would recite in what was becoming his anthem once he arrived from where he had just lost his job.

"You cannot keep losing jobs like this," Heaven said to her man time and time and again. It felt like the hundredth time she was telling him. It was becoming a trend and a rather bothersome one as well. Things slowly began to head toward a rocky path between the couple, with conversations becoming difficult, dialogue turning into accusations and angry words. Heaven slowly lost the sweet presence and comforting personality she had seen in Breezy as his frustrations grew. Their once hot and steamy affair slowly morphed into a bitter, cold, and emotionless one. Days felt long and unbearable, while nights felt impossible to navigate.

Breezy was definitely not the man she wanted him to be, and he didn't seem at all interested in becoming anything other than what he was. The difficulties associated with being poor were new to him; it came with struggles, suffering, and strife untold. He would lament and curse about his ordeals when daily reminders in the form of baby needs and family care came.

Heaven used to crave for and love the sound of her man coming home, but the pleasure had slowly worn off, and she seemed to find peace and solace in his absence as the days went by. She now resented everything about him, especially his broke ass. He had slowly transformed himself from a man she adored into one who constantly sought ways to irritate her. It definitely brought her mental hurt, having to cast her gaze into the blue eyes that used to melt her heart, only to find pain in it. The same blue eyes, which used to resemble Turks and Caicos beach water, now resembled fucking Sandy Point Beach water. It was beyond disgusting, or at least it was how she truly felt.

Heaven wanted more, more of life, and more for her daughter, if not for herself. She wanted everything she had dreamed of growing up, and not the adverse, which was her current case. She wanted more… more… more.

Soon enough, Heaven landed a new job working with her mother at Healthcare Associates International (HAI), while her mother reluctantly allowed Breezy to stay with them since he was Hillary's dad and she wanted Hillary to experience having a fatherly figure in her life.

The arrangement, which was undoubtedly an odd one, seemed okay at first. Heaven would go to work with her mother at HAI while Breezy would be tasked with nothing other than taking care of the house if he chose to. He didn't have to take care of Hillary, either, since they decided it would be safer and more appropriate to leave the baby girl at day care.

This gave Breezy room to do what he wanted when

they weren't home. His habit of littering the living room, leaving dishes unwashed, and even having friends over had slowly begun to boil tensions around the house. Heaven had continually managed to keep emotions in check, hoping Breezy would somehow be able to recognize his actions as wrong. Sadly, he just wasn't able to, and the day finally came when his straw would break the camel's back.

One Friday night, Heaven returned home from work in the evening, just as she often did, tired and disheveled from work. She walked into the living room, with Hillary in one arm, and was in absolute shock as she gawked at the rearranged furniture that could now accommodate Breezy's PlayStation addiction with his friends who had come over. He didn't seem to care about, or even notice that Heaven stormed off to place Hillary in her mother's room. Pacing around in anger and absolute rage, Heaven mumbled, "What on earth is going on with him?" There was just no explaining what he thought and why he did the things he did. His irresponsible acts around the house brought her serious concerns, and without showing signs that he was going to change, she realized there was a need to act. Heaven turned to her daughter and decided to keep the little girl occupied while she handled her father in the living room.

"This should keep you busy," Heaven whispered before playing a movie for Hillary. Heaven marched off to the living room determined to get her point across to Breezy.

"Breezy!" she screamed before seeing him.

He turned his attention to her briefly, bore nothing but a blank expression, and then turned around again to continue playing. Heaven could not believe he was ignoring her. After the torrid day of having to deal with customers and their bullshit at work, she wasn't expecting her man to compound her woes any further.

"*Why is he doing this?*" she asked herself without resolve.

There was just no getting through to him, and Heaven finally snapped. She stormed off, without Breezy noticing, to the kitchen. Heaven soon returned with a Breeze's favorite Turkey Hill iced tea, took a deep breath, and looked around the living room as those within it continued to ignore her existence. She stepped closer, stood before the television, and slowly poured the iced tea on the PlayStation. Breezy and his friends jumped up from the couch, looking frightened and obviously not expecting what she had just done. With a serious expression sprawled across her face, she said, "Get your white, no-job-having, broke ass up and out of my fucking house!" One after the other, his friends began to leave the house. She could see the sheer look of embarrassment on his face, but it was a long time coming. It was one thing being a lazy sloth around the house, and another thing bringing a bunch of friends like him with no job or purpose to come and mess up the entire house without even attempting to clean it up.

Breezy fumed red as he turned to look her in the face. "Is that what you want? You are kicking me out of your house?"

It was a daunting question and one that Heaven had never assumed she would answer positively until then. With a deep breath and a loud exhale, she replied, "Yes."

Breezy looked at her in disbelief.

"If this is as good as it is going to get, then it is best that your white ass leave."

Breezy looked back at her and lowered his head. "Every single time we have an argument, you end up bringing my race into it. I never mention yours."

He turned away, headed straight for the room, where his innocent daughter was enjoying some cartoon time, and stood by her bed for a while. His frowning face had mellowed into a smiling one now. He handed her some Twizzlers from by her bed and watched the little girl suck on them happily, before turning to look at Heaven.

"When you're done being a racist bitch, I will always be here for Hilly," he said. "This is the last time I am taking this bullshit from you."

With the words aired, he stormed out of the room, almost brushing Heaven with his broad shoulder as he walked past. Heaven walked over to the living room that he had been occupying. Amid the dirt and trash he left behind, he had not taken all of his things.

"Nah, you have to go with all of your shit." She shook her head as she raced to the bathroom. Heaven began to pack up all his things, hoping none would be left by the time she was done. She wanted no reminder of how much of a difficult man he was, and if it meant helping him do it, then it was precisely what she was going to do. While she tossed his things into a bag, packing them up and ensuring she didn't miss anything, Heaven did it with a heavy heart.

She definitely wasn't against him being around them, or even in their lives. She simply realized she needed to vent her frustrations and make them known as best as possible, or things wouldn't actually fall into place as she wanted them to. Tossing his clothes one at a time into a trash bag felt good and absolutely lovely, as she made sure she wasn't being sentimental about her actions for any reason. Even while she bore no intent to place any of his belonging in a dumpster, it still felt absolutely good.

"I am done with this," she said to herself through the ordeal, smiling sometimes and wearing a frown other times.

After finally packing almost all Breezy's belongings into one bag, she plucked Hilly from her bed and slowly curled into a ball to cry her eyes out. Her emotions were all over the place, and it was the only way she could actually express them.

"I trusted him with everything," she said to herself, recounting how she believed in Breezy and felt assured by him that they were going to be fine without his parents' money. She had hoped her existence would benefit from his wealth or whatever wealth he would amass from his family, only to be left flat-faced in insult and penury. Lifting Hilly up in her arms, she made the same promise all over again that she had made to her baby girl on the day she was born.

"I am going to succeed for the both of us," she assured her baby girl. "I will make things right by you and for you, I promise." Heaven continued to weep bitterly, unsure of how best to console herself or even her child, who had begun to weep.

"Mommy will give you everything… Mommy is going to love you more than life. Grandmamma will always be there for you." She sniffed. "We love you, and we will stop at nothing to make sure you have everything you need in life." She wiped some of the dried sugar off of Hilly's cheek and licked it from her thumb before placing a kiss on the baby's lips. There was no doubt in her mind about how much she loved her baby girl. She would stop at nothing to ensure they beat whatever odds life had to throw at them. She would make sure she provided for her daughter even if it meant toiling. Heaven was prepared to make something good of herself for her daughter.

"I love you to the moon and back," she whispered to her daughter and kissed her again. "It is just the two of us against the world." Then she sang.

"Just the two of us
We can make it if we try
Just the two of us
Just the two of us
Just the two of us
Building castles in the sky
Just the two of us
You and I."

Heaven sang the song proudly, reminiscing about how her mother would lift her up even in her early years, singing the same song to her. It was one of the most blissful moments while she was growing up, and being able to have the same experience with her daughter was precious.

Thoughts of the past made Heaven smile and momentarily forget about where she was and what she was about to do. The fact her name had been called still caused her jitters, as butterflies began to swarm in her belly. She tapped her feet into the ground in an uncontrollable manner, bit her lower lip, and continued to look around in an anxious manner.

Stating that she was nervous was an understatement. There was the possibility that everything might go wrong, and that alone would ruin years of lengthy waiting and planning. It would undoubtedly toss a wrench into her plans and cause her to uproot every single thing. Even while she was meticulous and organized in all her dealings and in her life generally, she still felt worried. Prior to her appointment, she had arranged everything she needed accordingly, followed the due process and instructions to the letter, which was one of the habits that had made her into an excellent employee over the years at HAI.

It had also gotten her recognition and performance awards. They finally called on her, and Heaven got on her feet, straightened her shirt, and breathed a loud sigh.

She made her way to the caseworker's office, knocked on the door, and stepped in to meet the sweet-sounding and kind-looking Indian woman. It brought Heaven's heart relief not having to deal with some bitch that would act and think the benefits being handed out were hers to give. "Kindly have a seat while I go through your paperwork," the lady said politely.

Heaven took her seat and slowly began to get anxious once again. There was no telling what could happen. She pondered hard and asked herself a butt load of questions about the processes and if she had done them appropriately. Her paperwork finally checked out, and her salary from HAI was well beneath the minimum salary requirements. The caseworker looked up at Heaven for a moment before proceeding to input her information into the database to ascertain if they were indeed true and correct. Within minutes, the result came through and they checked out accordingly. "Your documents were successfully verified," she said and looked at Heaven with a smile. She relayed where Hillary and Heaven would be assigned housing, with the monthly payment Heaven would pay as well.

Heaven gasped in shock and a feeling of excitement. It was the day she had looked forward to for so long, and she wasn't even sure how best to go about it. Living with her mom had been helpful, but it also came with its challenges. Issues had begun to arise with the manner in which her mother grew fond of Hilly. Her mother wanted to raise Hilly as she saw fit, without allowing Heaven be a part of her life as much as she would have loved to. In a bid to constantly keep the peace and continue to mooch off her mother, Heaven had begun to slowly lose her voice, but deep within, she longed for the opportunity to be her own woman and get her own place. She had figured it would curb a lot of disagreements with her mom and set new routines as best as possible.

The caseworker looked at the computer and slowly began to speak. "It looks like we have a two-bedroom basement apartment on Webster Street in North West, DC, for sixty dollars per month, available for move-in thirty days from now. How does this sound?" Heaven felt tongue-tied as she looked at the woman with glee in her eyes. "Well, it sounds good, but is there anything available on the Gold Coast, on Sixteenth Street?"

"No, not for a year," the caseworker replied. "If you don't take this place on Webster, your name will go back to the bottom of the wait list, and we have to begin the process all over again." There was definitely no room to wait another day. Heaven was desperate, but not in a bad way, though; she simply wanted a place to call her own and where she could raise her daughter.

"I'll take it."

She got the printed lease almost immediately and the move-in date was established right there and then.

"I believe we are done," the caseworker said with a smile on her face. Heaven shook hands with her excitedly and left. She raced to the bathroom, filled and drenched in anxiety, without knowing what to do in that moment. She slipped into an empty stall, took out the paperwork again as she sat on the toilet seat. She began to peruse the contents of her paperwork as best and as slowly as she could, hoping not to miss anything and to make sure there wasn't anything wrong with her newly secured space. It felt too good to be true; she had secured a nice place without facing hassles.

Definitely proud of herself and how she had accomplished this, Heaven jumped out of the stall, almost causing a lady who had walked into the bathroom a heart attack. Without a care in the world, she began to twerk, dropping it low as she backed it up into the bathroom stall. Her excitement was beyond containment.

Filled with happiness and excitement, she walked out of the building with the widest smile she had donned in years. Pulling herself together, she hailed a taxi and got in. Things definitely felt good, and for the first time in a while, she felt some measure of peace within herself. She felt unstoppable, refreshed in will and grit, and definitely determined to do more.

Tuning in the song best suited for the moment on her iPod, Heaven blasted "I'm Every Woman" by Whitney Houston as she rode in the backseat of the taxi and headed back home. "One down," she muttered to herself.

She knew there were many other issues still yet to be solved—finding love, getting a better job, and securing a stable life.

Chapter 3

The Climb

Heaven had never felt so many mixed emotions about something positive as she did when her moving day finally arrived. She paused, gave it a moment of thought, and took in deep but satisfying breaths as she gawked at the plans she had worked tirelessly for now slowly falling into place. It felt surreal and as if it wasn't ever going to be possible, but there she was, about to take the next necessary steps in her life.

It was the day to move into her apartment. The week before had been riddled with paranoia, endless questions inside her head, and the worry that things might possibly go south. For Heaven, things never always went as planned. At least, a perfect example was her episode with the father to her beautiful baby.

She had counted the days and noted every single thing happening until the move-in day finally arrived. To say she was excited was an understatement and an undeserved disservice to the lady. Her heart thumped, her breath felt heavy, and she felt a new wave of worry begin to descend on her as she approached the house.

There were issues to solve, no doubt. Moving into a new apartment is a huge commitment and a very big deal too. Change wasn't something she was comfortable with, and more so when the change had to do with planning and rearranging her life to suit a new directive or arrangement. Mentally, she felt prepared, but it was another story when it came to the physical side of things. She had the bedroom furniture from her mom's home and a few odds and ends, which she managed to pick up from Marshalls while she was waiting for the move-in date to arrive. The move was tedious but not as stressful as it would have been had she attempted to make the move by herself. Thankfully, her mother had asked a few brothers from the church to assist her in getting her things over to her new house. It was an immense weight off of her shoulders and one she was more than grateful for as she stood and watched them unload the items one after the other.

The time has finally come, Heaven thought. She wondered what she'd do first when she settled into the new apartment. She had a host of ideas in mind, and everything seemed juxtaposed against the other, without any one in particular coming to mind. She cringed with more feeling of anxiety and bit her lower lip as the boxes they unloaded lessened by the second.

I have a home, Heaven thought.

It was definitely surreal to think about, let alone begin

to believe. This was something she had constantly gone through and often wondered how it would feel not to have to continue depending on her mother or living with her. Being with her mother wasn't a bad thing, and it definitely wasn't a terrible idea, but there were restrictions, and that in itself was binding and troubling for Heaven.

More so, there was and had always been the need to be her own woman and create a niche for herself and for her daughter. The niche was now before her, and the possibilities that could come with it felt endless and unimaginable. "That's the last of the boxes, Heaven," one of the guys assisting her noted. Heaven looked at the moving truck and smiled. Her smile was wild; it stretched her lips from side to side, and she could feel butterflies in her belly, dancing around wildly as she thanked them for their assistance, one at a time. In the moment, while she showed her appreciation, her phone rang, and it was none other than Breezy. Holding her breath, wondering whether she should pick the call, she dallied for a moment before clamping her thumb down and hard on the "receive" button. "Hello," he said, coldly but with a hint that he was trying to disguise his emotion.

Heaven forgot she had mentioned her moving date to him. She wasn't on the verge of cutting him off entirely, since he was the father of her child and she still wanted his presence in her daughter's life, even if it was minimal. She held her breath some more, weighed her response before parting her lips to speak. Breezy cut through almost immediately and interrupted her. "Today is your move-in day, yeah? You got help already or you need me to come over with your unloading?"

Heaven was on the verge of scoffing, but it was bound to come off as rude. She understood his worry without doubt and knew why he was calling. There was no way in hell he was calling just to lend a helping hand. They weren't that jolly obviously, and knowing Breezy, his temper, and sense of jealousy, she knew he was simply trying to scope things out and ascertain answers to quench his insecurities.

Heaven thought of messing with him a little bit, but she had a lot to do, and the sooner the phone call ended, the better it was going to be for her. "No, I got it," she replied. "Everything is fine over here, and I don't need you to come help me unload. I got help already."

Her response was followed by a lengthy silence, but she could hear his breath continue to interrupt the silence intermittently. She figured he was weighing his thoughts, trying to decipher if she had help from another man and if he was being totally relegated. It was something she had gotten familiar with, and she knew too well how he thought and how his mind worked.

"What do you mean you got help already?" he asked in stern tone.

Heaven shrugged her shoulders as if he was right before her and replied, "It means I got help, and I really don't need you to come assist me."

She knew he wasn't going to come and help out. He was lazy and obviously would prefer gaming and sleeping or simply lying around to indulging in such tasking work.

"Who?" Breezy inquired.

Heaven shook her head in tiredness and lowered it. "I need to go. I'll speak with you later."

She brought the call to an end, turned to those who had helped her with her things, and thanked them again dearly. Breezy's call came through once again, causing Heaven to sigh in disbelief as she ignored it as best as she could. There was more work to be done, and she'd rather be focused on that than a man who was simply deluging her with phone calls to be sure she wasn't bringing a new man into her house or into her bed. Yet, his calls continued to come through, and she found herself compelled to pick up again.

"This is going to be a very busy day for me, Breezy. What do you want?"

"Send me your address," he demanded. "I want to come over in about an hour."

She scoffed, wondered if he was joking, but the tone with which he spoke definitely showed how serious he was and that he meant every word.

"I'll text it to you."

The call came to an abrupt end, and she forwarded the address to him. She wasn't about to cut him off; being Hilly's dad, he had the right to know where his daughter was living. "Thanks once again." Heaven waved at the guys as they got back into their truck and drove off.

A sigh of relief escaped her lips while she stood in front of her new apartment. The feeling was unbelievable and indescribable too. She took a good look around to be certain it was true, before making her way into her new home and gently closing the door behind her. A sense of empowerment came with being able to lock her door.

She looked around, tried to figure out where what will go where and what she still needed to get or to even make the apartment pop. There was still a lot of work to be done and a lot of things to buy, without a doubt. Her footsteps echoed as she walked toward the bedroom to check it out, and her heart sounded in loud thuds, too, as she stood by the bedroom door and imagined her daughter finally having a home. "This is fucking happening," Heaven said to herself. "This is definitely happening."

Tears rolled down her face from the corners of her eyes. She sniffed and wiped them off, but more came rolling down her cheeks in a show of how happy she was. She felt proud of not just herself but of the fact her mother had set her up on the right path to make the best possible decisions she could have ever thought of making for herself. About an hour later, still without touching a single box or unloading anything, three rapid knocks tore into her front door and almost startled Heaven into being frightened. She got up from where she sat, took slow walks to the door in curiosity before looking through the peephole to ascertain who was at her door.

Her initial guess was that neighbors around had seen her move in and possibly wanted to introduce themselves, but she was wrong. That white face was none other than Breezy, standing in front of her door, sweating profusely and looking as if he had jogged his way over, which caused her to smile a bit.

"Breezy?" She sounded as surprised as she was as she held open the door to look at him. Judging by how soon he had arrived, she wondered if he ran some red lights and stop signs on his way over. It wasn't above something he would do.

"Hey," he replied, trying to catch his breath. "I got you something."

He turned around and stepped to the side for her to see the truckload of items behind him. Heaven's eyes widened, her lips parted, and she sucked in a lot of air to show how shocked she was. Heaven looked away from the truck and back at Breezy for a moment, before looking past him again. It was obvious she struggled with being able to even come close to comprehending what was going on.

"What is this?" she asked in a shocked tone.

Breezy grinned like a schoolboy impressing his crush. "I got everything for you, babe."

She took another look at the truck and the amount of furniture he had brought over with him. It was well beyond anything she figured he could afford, let alone pay for with the money he didn't have.

"Oh my God!" she exclaimed as she walked past him

with her hands clamped over her mouth. "Where on earth did you get all this stuff from?"

It felt questionable, and she didn't want to be a part to anything that could bring problems in the long run.

Breezy waved her question away with his hand. "Don't worry about it. I have you covered."

His response still wasn't giving her what she wanted.

"What are you doing with all this furniture, and where did you get them from?" Heaven sounded persistent and wasn't about to let things go.

Breezy, regardless of his financial state had never stolen anything, or brought up the idea to do so. Heaven trusted him enough for that, even with his quirks. Yet it worried her to see such luxurious items that would cost so much. She stepped closer to examine them before turning to look at him and wait for a response. "You need to chill," he advised her. "I knew you'd need a lot of furniture in an apartment such as this, and I didn't want my baby sleeping on no messed up, shitty mattress." Heaven tilted her head to the side, obviously to question what he had just said. "That still does not answer my question, Breezy." Heaven pressed further. Seeing how evasive he was about the furniture items and their source bothered her. It left a sting at the back of her throat that she wasn't sure would go away unless she knew exactly where they were from and if it was safe to put them in her house. More so, there was the worry of messing things up before they had even begun.

The new apartment was meant to usher in a new episode for her and her baby girl. It was meant to be an opportunity to begin life anew without the fuck-ups from times past or the issues of the past meddling in any of her affairs.

"Will you chill the hell out?" he asked, sounding serious now as he stared right back at her.

Heaven shook her head and pointed her finger at the truck. "Are those things legit? Do I have to worry about our daughter every time I sit on them or make use of any of them? I need to know, Breezy, and you aren't stopping me from getting an answer if I will allow those items into this house." Heaven could hear herself sounding like a drama queen, but she wasn't about to ease off.

"It takes you nothing to answer the simple question, Breezy, unless…" She paused, knowing she was about to take things a step further if she completed the sentence. She had always trusted him, but a man in his shoes could be desperate enough to do anything, and it worried her. He clenched his fists on either side of his body, and with laden breath, closed his eyes before opening them again in readiness to speak.

"The furniture is fine, and nobody is coming back to confiscate it for any reason," he explained. "Trust me, I got them from a legit source, and I will never do anything to jeopardize Hilly or put you in—" Heaven held up her hand

and stopped his excessive talking. She wanted answers to her question, or she would stick to her guns to not allow any of the furniture in her house. It would be terrible running from the law when she was living in a building granted to her by her government. "I got a cousin who moved all the way to Paris to pursue modeling and does not plan to return anytime soon. She listed this furniture on Craigslist, but I asked her if I could use them for Hilly before anyone bought them, and she agreed."

Heaven felt it was odd, considering how much drama and turmoil they all had endured regarding his family and the color of her skin. She remained silent, but her disbelieving face and demeanor unsettled Breezy who couldn't look her right back in the eyes.

"I swear, shawty," he said, attempting to show he wasn't telling a lie. "She gave them to me, and mostly because of Hilly."

"Does she know we are black? Is she not aware of Hilly and I being black?" Heaven asked.

Breezy chuckled softly. "She actually thinks it's cool to be related to black people, and I can show you our text messages to prove it." He took out his mobile phone and showed her some of their conversations. By the look of things, his cousin loved Hilly and she was willing to let the little girl have everything without ever accepting a dime from Breezy. It was unbelievable and absolutely wonderful for Heaven, who could not hide her expression.

Such a random act of kindness was rare, almost

impossible, and it turned Heaven on in a satisfying way.

For once, it felt as if life was working out for her, and it felt absolutely wonderful to have Breezy's help. It wasn't something she experienced in the past, and she was absolutely certain he couldn't come to assist, but seeing him show up was unbelievable and exciting too. That side of him, which he was showing in that very moment, was all she ever wanted.

"I can help you move everything in, if you like," he offered.

She agreed without batting an eyelid. It would take him some time to get things done, and they spent the moment together, smiling and laughing without a single worry in the world.

"Is it okay if I spend the night here?" Breezy asked, rather politely and without any sense or feeling of entitlement.

Heaven looked around the house for a moment, turned to him and smiled. "Of course." The day had been perfect, and there was no reason for the night not to work out in such manner either.

Two days flew by fast, and while getting things into their proper space and places were tough, the mental strain accompanying everything Heaven wanted to achieve continued to come down hard on her like a blow. The nights had felt longer than usual, and even while Breezy had stayed over for the first night, she didn't sleep very well.

Being in a new environment often came with hassles for her, but her mind was wandering with other thoughts and for other reasons. For Heaven, securing an apartment wasn't all she wanted to do with herself, or even anywhere near the major goals she wanted to accomplish. It was nice having a place for her daughter, and with it came a sense of security as well.

Taking a deep breath, closing her eyes, and staring out her window from the dining space, she took in the surroundings. It wasn't as beautiful as those found in gated communities, but it was without a doubt wonderful to be enclosed in such wonderful space, she thought as she stared out into the distance.

"My housing is secured, what next?" she asked herself as she leaned back into the chair. Her mind raced with plans she had etched out for years, which were unfulfilled yet. Her goals were many and some seemed rather unachievable; most people might even call them goals of a dreamer, but she didn't care. She had a promise to fulfill, after all—the one she made to her baby girl. It was one promise she was going to fulfill even if it took the best of her.

She got up from her seat momentarily and soon returned with a notepad and a pen. With a mischievous smile on her face, which was meant to denote how serious she was, she bent over and began to scribble everything she had in her head. Doing so one at a time with intermittent breaks and pauses to try to think before noting down some more goals.

Within the next hour, she had scripted her short- and long-term goals across the pages of her notepad. Some looked tasking and daunting, but every single one seemed possible. Heaven trailed the list with her pen, hoping she had not missed anything at all as she settled on the first item on the list. It was one she knew might come off as stressful. but it was essential to anything else she wanted to do. "Clean up your credit report," she recited to herself with a smile across her face. She had done some research, and there were credit repair services willing to assist with the process, but with funds as tight as they were and her desire to learn the process rather than having to rely on people to sort them for her, she opted to fix it herself. It would possibly take her some time to read all she could about it and even consume a tremendous amount of time writing letters to creditors and awaiting response.

Regardless of everything else, there was one reason Heaven needed to fix her credit; she needed to get a job, and not just any job. She had her sights set on landing a government job; anything less wasn't going to be accepted, or it might be temporary while she continued to aim for her target. There was no other way she wanted it. She also wanted to own her own home in the very near future.

She shifted her notepad to the side and rested her elbows on the table while she flipped through her phone. It was time to place calls to those creditors in order to fix her credit.

Fixing her credit didn't come through as easy as she had expected. She understood a lot of hassles were bound to come with the ordeal, but it had taken longer than she had anticipated. Regardless, it turned out well, and Heaven took one huge sigh of relief as she walked out of one of the largest government contracting firms in the area, where she had applied for a new job. It was not what she wanted, but the larger paycheck was needed at that point in time. The interview in itself was awesome, challenging, and a sweet experience, just like the other two she had attended within the week. Responses from other employers she applied to had been encouraging, and she wasn't on the verge of stopping any time soon.

"I can pick the best and work with them," she continued to recite to herself when she placed her application through for job opening she read online.

Gone were the days of being dependent or having to believe in cashing out on other people's success. It was time to will herself into attaining what she wanted in life, and that was precisely what she was doing. The interview she just left had gone well, to the best of her knowledge. For some odd reason, which still baffled her, she liked having interviews. In fact, her mother had called her a serial interviewer. Unlike most people who shy away from interviews because they are often seen as strenuous, challenging, and mentally draining, it wasn't the case for Heaven. Being provided the chance to dazzle the interviewers with her charm, personality, and vast sense and use of vocabulary was something she wasn't about to let go to waste.

It was why she always took note of their expressions whenever she was being interviewed. It was refreshing to watch them become stuck in awe at her brilliance and even end up engaging her with so much respect and show of faith in ways most people in her past never seemed to do. Interviews boosted her ego every single time, and while she walked down the stairs outside the firm, she scrolled through her phone for her next appointment. She had just received mail from HAI, informing her that her position was being eliminated due to budget cuts.

Heaven smirked, shook her head, and sighed.

She wanted more, and she wanted the best—a federal government job was bound to provide her with ample benefits and money for proper training. It was why she had worked tirelessly and made certain to set her sights on doing whatever was bound to take her to land a government job. She had done her best to set things in motion by applying for vacancies she deemed would be effective.

Hurriedly, she weaved and marched through the street as the incoming crowd threatened to derail her steps. She had another interview slated for two o'clock, and it took almost an hour to get there. She hastened her steps and suddenly stopped in her tracks as her phone buzzed and got her attention. Curious as to who had sent her a message, she flicked through her phone and her jaw dropped.

To be certain of what she was gawking at, Heaven read through the message over and over again. It was a congratulatory mail informing her that she had been selected to work for a prominent law firm in downtown Washington, DC. -where her friend Michell had been working for years. "No," Heaven whispered in disbelief, but the words were right there before her. Elated and unsure of how to expel her emotions, she turned around, looked back at her phone, and read the words again. It felt like a dream, but one that was clear as day and undoubtedly made her day feel awesome already.

Confused as to what to do, with the email stipulating that she ought to respond within three days with her decision to accept the job offer or not, she dialed her best friend's line promptly.

Michell was the first person she badly wanted to share the good news with, then her mother, and Breezy will come next.

Chapter 4

Breaking the Law at the Law Firm

A week after she had received the email congratulating her on acquiring the job, Heaven arrived downtown and stood nervously before the Law Offices of Christopher Murphy. She couldn't quite contain how her excitement; her knees felt knocked and her belly felt full with butterflies as she clung onto her acceptance letter.

Her new duties had been described as complex, and while she stood there, imagining what she would be tasked with as the human resources assistant, she summoned every ounce of courage in her bones and marched right into her designated office. In there, the air and everything about life felt different and totally consuming. She paused, took a moment to breathe and some time to amass the fact that she was in a place many would kill to be in or to even become associated with.

The magnitude of what she was about to experience

had not struck her until she caught sight of her office, bearing her name engraved into a tile and neatly placed alongside a stack of notepads.

"Miss Heaven Davis" it had read, and with it came an undeniable feeling of joy. She approached her chair, plunged herself into it, and decided to get right to work. The day was about to be a long and daunting one, but one she was more than prepared to work through without having to worry or feel frightened. "Your job entails collating, being aware, and, at times, disseminating information regarding job openings, receiving candidate applications or resumes, as well as scheduling interviews," she had been told plainly and clearly.

It seemed easy, and her mind had immediately set out to make the best use of the opportunity she was granted. She had even gone as far as to discuss means to ensure that she would get the best out of having such knowledge of job openings.

"Here we go." Heaven smiled as she began to put her belongings into place.

It was a long day in the making, but one that she would soon acclimate to and continue in for the next few months until it became a part of her. In her current job, Heaven would soon come to realize how rarely jobs were made available at the law firm. However, an administrative position became vacant due to the previous occupant deciding to leave for another job elsewhere. Heaven landed the job. Michell had been working at this law firm since graduating high school and throughout college. Heaven, being the driven person she was, poke with Michell about the potential new opportunity, and her ever-encouraging friend encouraged her to quickly apply for the position before anyone else did.

Together, they would seek ways to not only scheme and plot toward ensuring Heaven would rise higher, but manipulate the entrance of resumes into the office.

Michell's agreed to shred any applications and resumes being submitted into the office for the administrative position, while Heaven's application would remain at the top without much competition.

"Do you really believe this is going to work?" Heaven had asked her friend on more than one occasion. Michell, with a mischievous grin replied, "Who always has your back and has never let you down?"

"You," Heaven replied honestly. "We should have a way of covering our asses. I don't want this shit coming to bite me in the freaking ass."

Michell stared at her friend as if she couldn't quite believe what was coming from Heaven's mouth. They always found ways to manipulate their way around things, and she never really heard Heaven complaining or even attempting to do so.

"Are you trying to be a bitch with me right now?" Michell asked. "You and I know there is no fucking gain without pain, so stop a being bitch about it and buck the fuck up!" As though she had been called to order, Heaven made no move or attempt to query what they were doing anymore. It was crazy as fuck, and it definitely spelled bad news for her or the both of them if anyone found out, but she wasn't about to let herself become fazed by such. It was even more troubling because they weren't sure if the documents were being sent in multiple copies to others in the office as well. "We ride, or we fucking die," Heaven muttered during one of their shredding sessions.

They had chosen a secluded office close to the back of the building normally for maintenance and was sparingly used. Armed with a shredder from her office, she would position the machine in the room, lock the door after most people had gone home, and begin the shredding activities without an ounce of sympathy whatsoever.

They blasted Big Sean's song *"I Don't Fuck with You,"* twerking to the lyrics. "I don't give a fuck, I don't give a fuck, I don't give a fuck!"

"Don't forget to separate out those who aren't feasible for the job," Heaven reminded her friend as they pored over the new entries for the week. She figured it would be easier to win against those applicants who were nothing special and whose experiences paled starkly in comparison to or with hers. It was the best way to stack the deck in Heaven's favor; regardless of how illegal their actions were, Michell didn't care a bit. Heaven was her ride-or-die bitch, and she would do anything and go to any lengths for Heaven.

"I still have one or more tweaks to make on your resume," Michell reminded her friend. "They are compiling everything we've been submitting in a week, and I cannot have you looking like a newbie."

Heaven nodded and felt grateful for having a friend like Michell who was very much willing to break the rules for her without a single thought whatsoever. Their scheme would get Heaven the job after getting called for an interview just some days after, with details of the job spelled out to her and assurances laid out in the most gratifying manner.

Nothing about her wrong deeds, the shortcuts, or the fact she had illegally attained the position bothered Heaven. For her, it was just another means to march on, and that was precisely what she intended to do.

Three Months Later

Heaven took in subtle but powerful breaths as she let them out without being sure of whether she wanted to walk into the office before her. By her watch, she had been standing in the same place for over a half an hour, and the situation didn't seem like it was about to change at all. She sighed once again, cursed her luck, or rather all she had done to be where she was.

Three months back, when it all began, she definitely felt the world had taken a turn for good on her behalf and that things were definitely about to fall in line.

Getting the job she rigged and that she made certain

others weren't eligible for or applications even processed had seemed like a good idea. There had been no telling signs about what she was about to face in the moment.

Until this job opportunity came through, Heaven had little to nothing to do in her previous office except answering phones, filing, and photocopying. Looking back in that particular moment, Heaven would pick that over what she was embroiled in at the moment.

On the surface of things, everything seemed perfect—getting a better work space, new office, new role, and obviously slightly higher pay. She could still remember the first time she walked into her new office to a loud gasp and an absolutely marveled expression on her face.

She placed a call to Michell to inform her of the development and the prospect of even being regarded as someone with higher authority than when she was a receptionist.

The first day was perfect, getting served Starbucks when she asked, being included in important meetings, and even being granted the opportunity to step in places she couldn't ever step into as a receptionist. Her work schedule was flexible too, and she had few people to answer to, but in there was where her major problem existed. Sadly, nobody had told her anything relating to the position she was newly appointed into. Nobody had been kind enough to warn her of the debacles associated with the position.

If Heaven been told, she was certain she never would have applied for the position. Her ignorance felt like a curse and a rather troubling one too. Her first of many experiences began with a day she had dressed up to create and leave an impression on her superiors. Pedro Perez, the male supervisor in charge of her unit, was one of the individuals she was to meet on that particular day.

He, having gone on a business trip for three days, had not been around when she started in her new position, but his arrival spelled trouble and exceeding trauma for Heaven even though she had not known at the time.

It began with his leery and soul-searching looks from where he stood, across the room from her. She had done her best to remain confident, look professional, and not shy away from his intense gaze, until she realized every single lady on the floor seemed to be distancing herself from him. With his gaze still on Heaven, he snapped his fingers at her and waved her over. "You'll be tagging along with me on my rounds for today."

Heaven's heart leapt with joy, and she could barely contain how she felt on the inside. Being granted the opportunity to learn from a superior sounded and felt like a good deal. It was one she couldn't pass on, and as she walked over to meet with him, she could have sworn she heard people cackling and mumbling incoherently.

Jealousy, she thought. It was all she could attribute their side chatters to be, and even while she stood by the man, she could still very much hear them continue to whisper.

"My name is Heaven." Heaven sought to introduce

herself; it was their first official encounter.

He smiled and waved off her hand before replying, "I know who you are. I handpicked you from your former post as the receptionist at HAI -- you were amongst a short list of applicants vying for your current position." She felt a tingle in her spine, and Heaven wished she had listened to it or even sought better clarification about whom she was dealing with. Somewhat naive, definitely buoyed to impress and feeling excited about the prospect of getting her job done, she watched him turn to her.

"I am Pedro Perez," he whispered before winking at her.

Heaven smirked inwardly, wondering if he knew what length she had gone to just to work with him. She couldn't help but feel smug about the fact she knew she had made her appointment possible, and contrary to what Perez, standing by her side, seemed to believe.

Michell and I got this job, she thought as the other managers began to march into the room.

It was obvious the executives respected Perez. Well, the men did and the women simply shot him some really troubling look. He sounded intelligent, direct, and charming; it was easy to listen to him speak all day long. Regardless, she saw nothing wrong—yet, at least—and decided to enjoy the ride as best as she possibly could. The meet-and-greet soon ended, and the executives and managers disappeared from the floor, but other workers who shouldn't even be on that particular floor continued to gawk at Heaven in a rather suspicious manner.

"Is this how tough things are up here?" she asked herself, trying hard not to care about them or whatever they had to say. She shifted to the side, caught Perez's eyes on her again, and this time, in a different manner than before. "Miss Heaven," he called out in subtle tone and flicked his finger at her, indicating she should follow him.

Heaven did as she was told, tailed her boss, and stepped into the elevator with him without asking where they were headed. Just before the elevator doors chimed close, she caught a glimpse of a lady standing in the hallway, shaking her head and lowering her face in a manner that meant she felt sorry. *What is going on?* she thought but remained silent.

The elevator doors chimed, and the air within the small cubicle suddenly thinned. Maybe it was because she could feel his eyes on the back of her neck, or simply because there was enough space to her left for them to stand side by side, and yet the Perez chose to stand directly behind her, but Heaven just didn't know. It left her nervous, though, and a little bit unsettled, but not anything big enough to cause her to feel absolutely uncomfortable. Well, that was until she felt him sniff her neck and slowly step away from her until he was now standing by her side again.

"You smell okay," he mumbled, somewhat disappointedly.

Unsure of what she had heard, Heaven cleared her throat and replied, "I'm sorry but I didn't quite catch that, sir."

Perez turned to her with a rather serious gaze and replied, "I said you smell nice but not good enough."

The words struck Heaven hard and gutted her deeply. She clenched her fists and felt a steam of embarrassment swell within her soul. Being labeled as someone who didn't smell nice wasn't something she ever wanted from a superior. Even while it felt odd that he stepped closer to sniff her, she still couldn't help but take his words to heart. Grinding her teeth and unsure of how to respond, she felt him slide his hand around her waist.

"You shouldn't beat yourself up. I will recommend something for you," he assured her. Everything he had done and that he was still doing was absolutely odd and baffling. His hand remained rested on her waist until the elevator doors chimed open and with it came a sigh of relief for Heaven. She felt like choking, and she wasn't sure she would still be breathing had the elevator ride continued for some seconds beyond.

"Thank you, sir," she finally replied with a bead of sweat rolling down her forehead. Perez cocked his head without turning around to look at her. "You and I are going to have so much fun." Fun definitely wasn't a part of what Heaven was looking for while working with him, but she nodded her head and decided to go along. He waltzed through the floor in no particular order, and ladies seemed to scatter away from sight systematically, almost like ants would around poisonous liquid. It was odd, to say the least, and even odder when the women began to shoot Heaven pitiful expressions.

"You can notice others on your own time, Miss Heaven!" Perez warned as he held open a door that led into an office for her.

She could swear every single person on the floor that she had walked through still gawked at her until the door slammed shut. Perez simply hummed and circled Heaven before walking over to his seat. She remained rooted some feet away from the desk placed in the center of the oval room. She took a moment to look around, taking into context how bizarre everything in there was, from the mahogany-colored table that bore odd drawings on its edges to the abstract paintings hanging on his walls, which she could swear bore some element of sexuality within them when you looked closely. A disturbing smirk now spread on the man's face as he said nothing and continued to look at her.

"What would you like me to do today?" she asked politely.

Perez took a moment to reply. "Nothing, my darling pumpkin…absolutely nothing." He reached for his desk and yanked open the first drawer, and Heaven could have sworn that she caught sight of some colored objects in there just before he shoved it back into place. He was holding a tiny can in his hand now, which he sprayed all over his body with the same disturbing smirk still implanted on his face. He tossed it in her direction and whispered; "Now you and I can be in sync."

Heaven looked confused, and her raised brow did enough to tell the man how confused she was. As much as it didn't stop her from catching the pink bottle half filled with perfume when he had tossed it, she still wasn't sure about what he wanted her to do with it. "I need you to wear this perfume," he replied. "Anyone and everyone who works with me knows what I want." Heaven nodded at the bizarre statement but said nothing to dispute it. "You may leave now, but when I call on you, I need you to come running," he said.

She nodded, short of words and lost on a response, before turning around and making her way to the door. Just as she reached for the door, she heard him speak.

"A shorter and tighter skirt will give your ass much better shape than what I can see from here." It was the highlight of the Perez's oddity, and without a single word she exited the room. Heaven could not believe it when she heard herself sigh in relief and aloud. She looked up to the smirking and pitiful faces of the workers on that floor looking right back at her.

"This is definitely the weirdest day and experience I've had with any of my managers," she said to herself, while doing her best to become distracted from those around her.

"If only she knew," one lady said before shaking her head as Heaven walked past.

"There is no way out for her now," a man said.

They seemed to be hinting at something she couldn't

quite pick up. To the best of her knowledge, it had something to do with Mr. Perez, but she chalked it up to them talking about the man's idiosyncrasies and nothing major. She glanced at bottle of perfume in her hand and shook her head. It was definitely one bizarre day, and she could not quite wait to share it with her friend.

Michell would always listen, and that in itself was good enough for Heaven as she returned to her office on that odd day. The rest of the day would trickle by with nothing else of importance occurring.

That same evening, Heaven stretched her consciousness away from her room while she sipped from her glass and barely paid any attention to the other person in it with her. She still could not help herself, as events of the day continued to race through her head. In spite of the episode with Mr. Perez, the day had been okay by the standard of things. Yet, she could not help but feel worried by the manner in which people continued to linger their gazes on her. It had been baffling, troubling, and somewhat bizarre. "Don't tell me you got my ass sitting here while you get lost in some thought." Michell's voice broke through, causing Heaven to snap back into consciousness. For a moment, she had forgotten she was with her. The plan for the night was to drink and celebrate Heaven's new position since they had not really had the opportunity to do so over the week since she got hired.

Heaven smiled back at her best friend and replied, "Sorry, I was just occupied by one crazy thing I went through today."

Michell moved to the edge of her lounge chair and looked at her best friend with a concerned look spread across her face. "Does it have to do with the new job or is someone trying to bust your balls?" Michell asked. "You know you cannot allow anyone to hassle you or even bitch-slap you in that office?" Heaven nodded her head and gently set down the glass in her hand before replying. "It has nothing to do with that, but I think my new supervisor is weird."

Michell stiffened a bit but seemed to compose herself almost immediately. She shrugged her shoulders as if she didn't see anything wrong or even feel anything was wrong before returning to her drink. "Are you listening to me?" Heaven asked her friend, who was definitely acting weird.

"Come on, girl. You're just starting in a new place, and of course managers will differ, and you have no idea what I went through when I first started in that same law firm," Michell explained. "I don't think it is anything to worry about."

Heaven keyed into her friend's words and nodded her head. She figured she'd simply go with whatever flow her new office brought her, and hopefully she could see another opening to further herself and her cause. Being promoted wasn't the target point, and it definitely wasn't about to hinder her from furthering her plans.

"So, tell me about Breezy, and let's put away this office talk for now, please."

Michell desperately sought to change the topic. "How are you guys coping with Hilly in the middle of all this?"

It was a subject Heaven had pondered hard about over the past few weeks. "I drop her off at the day care center, and he comes around to visit when he can,"

Heaven replied without putting too much into it. "We will be fine." They both cocked their heads and continued sipping from their glasses in silence. Well, Heaven's mind bore no silence, and the more she allowed herself to think, the more disturbing she found the fact that her superior, had given her his half-used bottle of perfume to use.

Did he mandate that I make use of it? she thought, confused. *Or am I overthinking this?* Heaven felt stuck, and she had never found herself in such a position before. She sighed aloud and intermittently before finally deciding to enjoy girls' night and not ruin it with her incessant overthinking.

"I must be imagining things," she said to herself. "Perez is just queer." She'd rather chalk it up to that and with another sigh, she finally found relief.

"So, what's up for tonight?" Michell asked.

They would end up spending the entire night playing a game or two, with gossips and gist on what was going on around the office and in the lives of others they knew.

    Heaven returned to work the following day, beaming, and a smile on her face, waving at everyone who crossed her path and determined to make the best of her new opportunity. She marched her way out of the elevator and headed right for her office, when she spotted the door opened, and oddly so. Momentarily stopping dead in her tracks, she looked around for others, but she seemed to be the only one on the floor. Slowly, she approached the door before pushing it open to see the beaming face of none other than Pedro Perez seated on her chair, legs crossed on her desk, and with a smile on his face. He glanced at her without a word, before running his eyes along her entire body in a provocative manner. "Right on time." He giggled before taking his feet off of her desk.

    Heaven glanced at her watch and noted she was half an hour early. "Good morning, sir."

    He raised himself from the chair and began to head her way. "Yeah, good morning." He paused some feet away from her, suddenly wore a frown, and stepped closer before circling her like a vulture. Heaven felt nervous and absolutely uncomfortable as well. She cringed and held her breath while he stepped closer to sniff her hair without uttering a word yet. "Is something wrong?" she asked, doing her best not to stammer. Perez shook his head almost as if he was disappointed before replying,

"What is it going to take you to smell nice and the way I want it?" His question definitely worried her, and it felt worse when she felt his fingers sneak into her hair while he seemed to be toying with it. His warm breath tickled her neck as he stepped closer, and she could swear he was sniffing her hair. "A fine-looking ass like you have to smell nice." Heaven started to speak, to inform him that she wore perfume, but chose against it as he continued to toy with her hair before resting his hands on her shoulders. She felt disturbed by the fact he seemed comfortable staying behind her. She wished he'd stand in front of her so she could take note of whatever it was he was doing.

"Use the perfume I gave you, and get the documents I dropped off on your desk ready within the next hour," he demanded before running his hands down her shoulders, toward her arms and then halted them just some inches away from her waist. He purred, took in a heavy breath, and seemed to exhale in satisfaction before turning away and leaving her office. The moment the door slammed closed behind her was a moment of relief for Heaven; she could not help but exhale aloud as well. She had intentionally not used the perfume he gave to her, but judging by the looks of things, she had no choice but to use it now. Retrieving the perfume from her bag, Heaven helped herself to some sprays as the air immediately got filled with the scent of lavender and other fragrances she could not quite decipher.

"Anything to make the manager happy," she recited to herself as she sprayed some more of the perfume. She dived right into rounding off the task Perez had brought over to deliver within the hour as asked. Done with her work, she headed right for his office and met his absence. She dropped the files on his desk, turned around, and almost had a heart attack as she caught sight of him now standing before her with a grin on his face. "You are beautiful," he muttered while he motioned to reach for Heaven's waist with both hands. Slowly and surely, she wiggled her way out of his grip before stepping to the side, hoping he wasn't going to follow her. "I can really be of help with your career in this firm and outside of it as well," he continued. "Just do what I say, when I say it, and listen to what I want, and everything will be all right."

Confused as to what the hell he was talking about, Heaven remained silent but wary of Perez and his fingers. He drew closer and finally managed to lock her body close to his as Heaven grew in distress and feeling of anxiety. "You smell perfect, and I have to confess to personally handpicking you when I saw how cute your ass was."

Heaven unlocked herself from his grip, took some steps backward, and watched the man slowly begin to sniff the hands he had wrapped around her waist as if he was trying to savor the scent. "Is there anything else you'd need from me today, sir?" she asked politely, hoping to make her way out of his office as soon as possible.

Perez nodded. He turned around and walked toward the door to ascertain it was locked before turning around to look at Heaven. "I want you to dance for me," he said.

"What?" Heaven was shocked and confused. He nodded his head as he headed over to his seat and settled into it. "Come on. Don't be shy… Dance for me, twerk for me… It is all in good fun and nothing else."

Heaven was definitely not about to demean herself for a man she was beginning to sense was nothing more than a sexual predator of some kind. She'd rather try to make her way out as soon as possible, but she wasn't quite sure on how to go about the process. "I'm sorry, sir, but I don't dance," she lied. It was the best she could say. The simple fact was that she was a remarkable dancer, just as Michell was. There was no way they both wouldn't know how to dance, considering the sort of life they lived. She just wasn't about to do anything remotely close to making herself look or feel like a cheap trick before her seriously nauseating manager.

"You are going to make things hard between us, aren't you?" he said. "Well, it is fine if you don't dance." Heaven sighed in relief.

"I need you to photocopy those documents and make six copies of each," he instructed. "I need them by noon." The files contained no less than thirty individual pages, and she had a feeling that Perez was trying to punish her for not doing what he had asked. For Heaven, it was far better than having to dance in an environment meant to be of professional standards for a man who didn't seem to have every screw in his head in place.

"Sure," she replied before picking up the files and

marching her way out of his office. She couldn't help but feel relieved. Being away from him and breathing a different air from the one he was made her feel happy within and jubilant as well. The stares still lingered on her when she walked past, and she could sense those working around the office had something or some things to say they weren't letting out.

Michell said he is all right, she thought. Since her friend had been working there longer than she had, she figured Michell had to be right, after all.

"Just do your work and everything will be fine," she said to herself. All she wanted was the pay and any other way to further herself on the hustle chain. Her aspirations had only begun, and she hoped to soar higher and get better in time, and that was exactly what she was going to do. While walking over to the photocopying room, Heaven had pictured herself seated in three different offices, with no less than a thousand employees dancing to her tune. It felt good, and it definitely made her feel happy about herself. She no longer bore the mind-set of a victim, and it was nice to see her mind soaring with positive thoughts.

"All for Hilly," she reminded herself before placing the huge file in her hand atop the photocopying machine. "Sweet!" Seeing there was no line in the photocopying room, she set about her business as fast as possible, humming to herself to drown out the boredom and silence. Minutes trickled by, and events of the day seemed to slow down. She managed to finish only eighteen copies, when she felt a pair of hands around her waist and a warm breath pressed against her neck as well. Heaven's skin seemed to jump off her bones as she turned to see Perez with a finger to his lips, indicating she needed to keep quiet and not make a sound.

"What on earth are you doing?" she asked, hoping he would leave her the hell alone. "Appreciating how sexy your ass looks in this fitted skirt," he replied. "I see you took to my advice, and I must confess that you look ravishing." If there was any look on Heaven's face, it was one of despair and discomfort all wrapped into one.

"I have work to do," she reminded him. "This is also highly inappropriate for the workplace – it's inappropriate and unwanted period."

Perez didn't seem to care; he shrugged, stepped closer, and planted a peck on her cheek. His manhood quite prominent through his slim fit pants. Heaven's skin crawled with discomfort, and her breath became heavy and troubling. She clinched her teeth as her eyes were red. "I knew I made the right choice in picking you." He smiled at her, just before someone began to pound on the door to the room, which the Perez had locked without Heaven even noticing. Hurriedly, she raced to the door, breaking away from his gaze for a second before gladly opening it to let whoever was on the other side to come in. A young man stood by the door, casting weird glances at Heaven and Perez before slowly making his way into the room.

"I guess I'll be seeing you later," Perez said before exiting the room. Heaven wished the young man had come to knock on the door sooner. She felt violated, abused, and without words to express her pain.

"Are you okay?" the guy asked, looking suspicious and worried for her. Heaven did what she knew was best for her in that moment if she wanted to keep having her job. "Yes, I'm…I'm fine," she lied. She rushed to complete her task, all the while wondering what she could do to make the harassment stop.

A month after the incident in the photocopy room, Heaven had managed to steer clear of Perez even though it was an almost impossible task to do. Instead, she found ways to avoid being alone with him, or being in any secluded situation with him, regardless of what she needed to do or what was expected of her by her manager.

The rules were simple; ensure the doors are open at all times, never get into the same elevator with him, and if she could, she always stayed with her back against the wall, or made sure they boarded an elevator with others, and reduce the number of times she had to frequent his office. She had the urge to speak with Michell about the new developments, but she was certain her best friend would brush it off as nothing. More so, it wasn't an odd thing for superiors to flirt with their employees or for them to make glances and passes at them often. The disturbing fact about Pedro Perez was the fact he wanted to touch her at every chance he could muster.

His endless compliments about her ass and the manner in which he said her shape was mesmerizing had heightened over the month, but she had restricted herself from being in any position or situation where he would be able to lay a finger on her.

One morning while she made her rounds, Heaven stopped by the assistant secretary's office, hoping to get some much-needed documents essential for a meeting meant to happen by noon that same day. She knocked on the office door and was granted entrance by a squeaky feminine voice coming from within the office.

"Come right in," she had said.

Heaven did as she was asked and stopped at the sight of the extremely petite lady seated behind her office desk.

"Good morning, my name is Heaven—" Heaven sought to introduce herself but got interrupted almost immediately. "No need for an introduction, I know who you are," the secretary said with a bizarre smile, with the right corner of her mouth. "Everyone in this firm knows who you are, just as we knew the others and will end up knowing whoever comes after you."

Heaven looked around the room, wondering if she was the one the petite lady was referring to or if there was someone else in the room. "You work under Pedro Perez, don't you?" she asked. Heaven nodded her head. "Then we know you, and you are definitely the one I'm talking about," the woman reiterated and affirmed her point again.

Heaven's chest felt heavy, and her eyes narrowed seeking to understand the secretary's angle. She wanted to know what the woman meant, but she sensed she wasn't about to get anything else out from her, or she wouldn't have been speaking in such a cryptic tone.

"All I can say is what I told the last pretty lady he hired, just like you," the petite lady said as she got on her feet. "Be careful." She handed Heaven the file, and Heaven watched the lady head out of her office without uttering another word.

There are crazy people in this office, Heaven thought as she watched the woman leave. She was definitely bent on finding answers now, and she would go about seeking them as best as possible. Something doesn't feel right.

She wished she knew what it was and how to combat the mystery. To the best of her knowledge at the moment, Perez had the nasty habit of attempting to touch her and utter inappropriate things, but nothing else caught her attention.

More so, Michell would or should tell her if there was a problem, and considering her best friend assisted in helping her land the job, she figured there was nothing else to whatever was going on.

Don't get frazzled, baby girl, the inner voice in her head warned. *Whatever this is, you can beat it*.

Heaven believed all she had to do was be diligent in her work and simply stick by the rules she just put into place regarding Pedro Perez. Something about him still worried her, though, and she understood she would be lying to herself if she claimed otherwise. Troubled in mind and definitely drenched at heart, she went through the day reeling in thoughts and drowning in guesses as to what she had gotten herself into.

Chapter 5
The Biggest Sexual Harasser Ever

For Heaven, while the weeks continued to trickle by, nothing about being in her current situation made sense. Aside from donning the badge that said she was now one of the higher-ups or that she worked in a place that could be regarded as better in comparison with her previous job, nothing else was of fancy to her, and for one particular reason—Pedro Perez.

The man continued to grow in his disgusting character, causing her mental struggles, and some degree of paranoia slowly became attached to her ability to focus around work or to even attempt to become comfortable in his presence. Each day dragged along in the same manner, and when she finally got home, she still had to contend with varying thoughts on his actions and what he might do to her.

Breezy thankfully had not added to her stress and keeping his distance somewhat had helped, but Perez was always in the picture.

While she stood by the kitchenette in her apartment, staring at the coffee mug in her hand, her mind wandered back to events of the day. She could recall the meeting she'd had that morning with Perez and how her entire body felt like there was a target being placed on her back. His eyes, forever drilling, and the inappropriate expressions on his face had made things worse and unbearable.

Can he stop? she thought. It was a genuine question for which she struggled to produce the right response. If only there was a way to know whether he was going to stop. So far, so good, as he had limited his acts to when she was around him at the office, and she was grateful. It meant when she was at home all she had to worry about was her daughter and how their lives would move forward. So, there she was, partly drained by the day's activities and partly consumed by what the night would be and how morning would slowly sneak up on her as it had done over the past few weeks. Being a single mother was stressful in its own right, and having to do so with such a demanding job was equally daunting. It made her wonder if she could continue with strength, or if she might fall apart eventually.

While she struggled with her thoughts, she turned around to the beeping sound from her cell phone. It was indication that she had just received a text message. Walking over to retrieve the phone in a nonchalant manner, she scrolled through and flicked on the messaging app to see the somewhat foreign contact.

Who is this? Heaven thought before slowly finding a

place to settle and sit in. Slowly, a word at a time and with her focus drenched in the messages, she began to make out the individual who could be responsible for the message. It caused her insides to boil, her hands to tremble, and her eyes to narrow as her lips wouldn't dare read the distasteful and annoying words out loud. His audacity was pure and raw. His nonchalance and lack of respect for her privacy were obvious and clear as day.

"That bastard!" she fumed, tightening her hand around her phone, almost crushing it. She could not believe her eyes and the audacity behind Pedro Perez messaging her after work. She had done well enough to avoid conversing with him outside of work. He had even managed to offer her a ride more than once, and she declined. The last thing she wanted was a man of his questionable sanity showing up at her doorstep every now and then, or even at all.

"Why is he doing this?" she asked aloud. It was the first time she had found herself in such a situation where a man would continue to harass her with no reprieve. It was disgusting and definitely infuriating, and the more she thought of it, the more troubling it was. *I need to keep Michell informed*, she thought before scrolling through her phone. Taking a quick pic of the chat, she sent them to her best friend, hoping for a supportive response or some insight into how best to handle the man troubling her. The wait for a response from Michell was long, and Heaven was beginning to wonder if her friend even wanted to reply, before the single word came through.

"LOL," was all Michell could muster.

Heaven read the response again and again and again until she found herself with a headache. Michell obviously, and for reasons she couldn't fathom, didn't seem to care about whatever was going on. Heaven chose to chalk it up to her being involved in something or engaged in a consuming activity of some sorts in that period.

Without notice, her hand shuddered as the phone in her hand began to vibrate vehemently with a call. The caller ID sprawled out the same number she had received text messages from, and immediately her stomach sunk badly.

She clinched her teeth and felt an uncomfortable warm air suddenly swallow her, before hovering her thumb atop the "receive" button, wondering whether she ought to accept it or decline. The call finally and thankfully dropped, bringing her a sigh of relief before it came through again, almost immediately. Heaven wanted nothing to do with the Perez outside of work, and if she had her way, she'd prevent him from ever calling her. Yet she felt stuck, and knew if she didn't pick up, it might come off as being rude. "Hello," she whispered upon receiving the call, with her breath heavy and her hand still shaking tenderly. Silence ensued for a moment, and she wondered what games he was playing, or if he wanted to speak with her at all. "Hello, Heaven." She groped the arm of her couch with her left hand, shook her head, and closed her eyes as she felt some audacious wind rush out from her windpipe. *Let him speak, but say nothing*, she cautioned herself as she felt a swell of anger begin to rise inside of her.

Perez spoke again and clearly this time around, "Hey, babe."

"Babe?" she said, without realizing she just spoke. A degree of anger followed the tone with which she spoke, and she couldn't quite fathom what exactly to say or how exactly to continue indulging him. Her throat felt stiff as she pondered hard on her next words, but it seemed like he was just warming himself up.

"Yeah, I waved at you at the park when you were leaving tonight, hoping we could share the night out and maybe even get some." He chuckled naughtily before clearing his throat and continuing. "You know what I mean." Heaven prayed for grace and the strength not to lash out at the despicable being attempting to make her life a living hell. "I really don't feel comfortable doing this, and I wish you'd stop," she said respectfully. He took a long pause, breathed into his phone more than twice before replying. "You're a grown-ass woman with a freakishly sweet booty I am sure will be tasty between my—"

She didn't let him complete the sentence, bringing the call to an end with a sigh of relief. Hearing his voice was traumatizing, and having to struggle through the process of listening to him was even more difficult. "Oh God!" she yelled before ramming her fist into the couch in disgust. It was terrible enough to be harassed, and then it had to be a slime ball in the frame of Pedro Perez, and sexually, no less. She needed a way out, and that looked to be the only way she would be able to survive working with the man.

"Avoid him, and you'll be fine," she recited to herself as she watched her phone. It began to ring again. The man was obviously tireless in his pursuit and without doubt an absolute maniac in his actions. She turned off her cell phone, checked on her daughter, who was still sound asleep in bed, and with a heavy set of eyes and a heavy heart, Heaven hoped and prayed that the following day would be far better than the one she had.

She never would have guessed her day would end with the slime ball Pedro Perez being the last person she would speak with. It didn't feel like a good omen for whatever would come her way the following day. Regardless, she'd let the night wane, and pray morning light would wash everything she dreaded away.

Sadly, Heaven could still recall everything that happened the night before as though it was happening right before her. It had taken her hours to pull out her cell phone, but she didn't still want to have it around her as she made her morning rounds. It was Friday, after all, and most people just couldn't wait to get off work by noon, but not her.

Owing to the simple fact that life for her had wound down from the extravagant fun-loving persona into the more serious-minded one she was, Heaven was bound to spend her night in bed, chatting or maybe simply playing with her daughter. It was her new routine, and one she would often look forward to after work. Therefore, Friday nights were no different.

The next day

"Good morning, Heaven," she heard someone greet her from behind, just before the hairs at the back of her neck stood. Slowly, she turned around to the smiling face of Pedro Perez, just before he walked out of sight and veered into his office.

"Not so good a morning for you, is it?" a male cleaner straightening his earpiece said to her with a chuckle. The young man, who was quite popular among those working in the office, returned to his task, but Heaven sought him out and approached with the intent to know whatever he knew or if there was a way to avoid the nonsense she was being dealt.

"Mark!" she called out.

Mark paused, unhooked his earpiece, and wrapped it gently around his neck before staring at Heaven with his deep-blue eyes.

"What's his deal?" she asked.

Mark looked over her shoulder and then back at her. "I'm sorry, but I don't think I understand what you're talking about." He turned away, motioned toward resuming his work, but she hindered him by shoving aside his bucket. She wasn't about to be ignored, and especially not when she knew that others around the office weren't interested in speaking with her about Perez or about whatever was going on with the man. Mark seemed hesitant, and his body movement and language got Heaven wondering how much he knew. He looked around worryingly and then settled his gaze back on her with a frown. "What do you want to know?"

"Why won't anyone talk to me about him?" she asked directly.

"Nobody goes against Pedro, and especially not good-looking ladies who he brought into the picture to be his play toy," he replied. "You of all people should know better, considering Michell has worked here longer than even I have." It was all he was willing to say before he turned around and continued his work. His words definitely left Heaven confused. Michell had told her nothing, and she didn't understand what he meant by being Pedro's play toy. To the best of her knowledge, he was just a creepy guy, but hearing he made a habit out of it sunk her stomach.

"Heaven!" His voice stood tall and in commanding tone as he called out to her.

Reluctantly and with no choice but to heed his call, Heaven replied and slowly began to make her way over to where he stood, his hand extending his office door open for her to walk in. Slowly, with different thoughts encroaching the already muddled space within her mind, Heaven did as she was told and stood with her back away from the man and her attention solely focused on him.

He slammed the door shut behind him, turned the

key, and placed the shunt into place before turning his attention to her with the most disturbing grin appearing wildly on his face. "I had the best sleep last night, and do you know why?" he asked. "Hearing your voice brought about some soothing and emotionally calming feeling for me."

"That makes one of us." She sighed as she mumbled softly to herself. She would rather the night and the incident that came with it didn't occur. In fact, she stayed up until some minutes after three in the morning before finally falling asleep. His voice wasn't just haunting, it was tormenting. The audacity behind his act had caused her some degree of distress as well, and having to stand before him while he recounted the ordeal made her wonder what sort of audacity he was operating with.

"Well," he said, walking past her and settling into his seat. He held out his hand and waved her over to one of the two empty seats before him. Heaven wished she could decline, and for the same reason she was wearing his nauseating cologne, she found herself taking the seat he offered with a bogus smile on her face.

"What exactly do you want?" Pedro Perez inquired with a grin.

The ambiguous question left her perplexed and without a response for the first few minutes. "I'm sorry, but I don't get your question," she replied sincerely.

He leaned back into his chair and rephrased his question into much better light. "What do you hope to achieve while you work here?"

Heaven slowly opened her mouth and wanted to get her words out but felt some degree of restraint as she looked into his eyes. Nothing about him seemed natural, and she worried he had an agenda, which she just wasn't sure of yet. She decided to simply shrug, sound nonchalant before replying, "Hopefully become a better person and gain more recognition."

He shot her a staunch look, almost as if he struggled to reconcile her words with common sense or whatever he had in mind.

"Well, I went through your profile again last night, you know, when I was thinking 'bout you." He licked his lips annoyingly rather than seductively before continuing. "I can tell you're a lady with serious ambition, and I would love to help you achieve many of them." His words seemed to tease Heaven's interest a bit, and she moved to the edge of her seat with a smile. "How so?" she asked.

He winked at her, placed a finger to his lip, and kissed it in a bizarre manner before getting up from where he sat.

"For starters, you could invest some of your time in and with me," he said outright.

Heaven pretended as though she didn't quite know or even understand what he was talking about and started coughing like she was choking on ice. "I am a tad lost," she said.

He rounded his desk and settled behind her with his

hand slowly reaching for her shoulder as he spoke. "You know… You and me…"

Heaven shrugged her way out from his grasp and got on her feet. His disturbing cologne aside, his hand felt rough on her skin, and everything about him standing behind her was just badly creepy. "I would like to leave now," she informed him with a frown. "Why? Are you offended?" She ignored him as best as she could, stormed off, and helped herself with the door, before slamming it behind her and disappearing from sight. The farther she got from his office, the better she felt; she didn't want to stop walking until she got into the restroom. Eyes filled with anger and with every single nerve in her body screaming for her to take action, she walked over to the faucet and splashed water on her face.

"Calm your nerves," she whispered to herself. "Calm your nerves and don't allow that weirdo to get the better of you." Copious amounts of blood rushed through every single vein in her body, and while she stood before the mirror, all she could see and feel was the distasteful presence of Pedro Perez. She cringed and sighed for the umpteenth time, praying she wasn't going to lose it. She needed the job, and she definitely needed the experience to build on the limited work experience.

Yet, there was the wonder about Michell and what Mark the janitor had said.

According to him, her best friend should know better about Pedro Perez the animal, but she couldn't figure out why Michell was withholding this critical information. "You can overcome his bullshit," she reminded herself. She had come so far, and she was not on the verge of allowing herself to crumble under situations many women have successfully gotten out from over the years.

She recognized the fact that she was not the first, and she was willing to abide by that. She slowly edged herself away from the mirror with a better and more relaxed look. "You've got work to do," she reminded herself before turning around.

Exiting the restroom, she felt better, walked better, and even managed a smile or two at those around her until she arrived at her desk, where the disturbing sight of files piled atop one another broke her spirit. "A little something to keep your Friday busy," the note sticking out from one of the files read in black ink with Pedro Perez's handwriting as visible as day. The stacks of files couldn't be done within the hours designated for work.

To make matters worse, she was certain she wouldn't be able to finish within working hours, even less of a chance to do so on a Friday when there were fewer hours available to work. His resolve was stunning, to say the least, and the measures he would go to was baffling.

"If this will keep him from harassing me, then I guess this is the way to go," she said to herself with a slight frown. Making her way to retrieve the work before her, Heaven soon realized they were mostly tasks not even meant for her or her office. She was being punished for being daring enough to rebuff the cologne-loving Pedro Perez. Feeling somewhat relieved and regretful, she slumped into her seat and set right to work.

She proceeded with the first file, all the while cursing under her breath while attempting to shuffle through it all before nighttime would fall upon her.

Getting her daughter from day care and ensuring she was well cared for before going to bed was part of her worry, but Perez didn't seem to care.

"That son of a bitch!" she snapped while tossing a file to the farthest corner of her office. Heaven was frustrated, and nobody seemed intent in assisting her through the melee. It became apparent that she would have to handle things by herself and without any assistance.

Five hours passed, and it felt like five years. She toiled and drowned in the workload, and before she knew it, time had completely left her behind. The soft taps on her office door brought her back into consciousness of her surrounding, as well as how much time she had consumed while she sorted Perez's work. "Someone is busy." Michell chuckled oddly before stepping into the office. Heaven held her arms open to signify how much she had to cover and how many she had done so far. "Pedro Perez is tripping or something. That dude has me doing work when it's not even my goddamn business."

Michell accessed some of the files and snickered. "Well, it means no Friday night out for you. The other guys are thinking of drinking at Palms, and I'm going too."

Heaven nodded and chose to take her mind off of

whatever fun they might be having, since she had to finish up in time and get home.

"Just be you and do what he wants," Michell said as she turned around and left.

Do what he wants? Heaven thought. She felt confused and wasn't quite sure about what her friend meant. "Something is definitely wrong with that bitch," she thought out loud before facing her work again.

Soon enough, within minutes of Michell exited the room and the entire floor clearing out, a similar knock rattled her door.

"Who the fuck are…" she raged before realizing she was in a work environment and that such words weren't appropriate.

Perez stood by the door, arms folded and his eyes fixated on her as though she owed him something.

"Nice choice of words," he teased.

She could swear her dislike for him was only growing, and the longer he pressed and pushed her patience, the more she wanted to ram whatever object of valuable weight in her surroundings into his head.

"How's the task coming?" he asked while he rolled up his sleeve to have a look at his watch.

Heaven refused to respond, citing how many files remained untouched and how much more she needed to work if she wanted to leave within the next three hours.

"You know I have a thing for you, don't you?" he asked as he proceeded into the room. "Something about your ass in those tight skirts just makes me…hmmm."

Heaven caught sight of the wedding ring perfectly lodged around his finger and wondered what sort of woman would have chosen to marry someone in the frame of such an animal.

"You can be the queen in these halls, and I can personally guarantee you some really solid promotion if you simply dance to my tune."

She wished she could do as he was saying, but sadly she couldn't. He was asking for way more than she could give, and worst of all, his entire being and existence was appalling.

"What would you say to dinner and you not needing to do any of this tedious work anymore?" He smiled.

Heaven gave no impression that she was trying to think about it. She replied staunchly, "No."

The look on his face explained how his ego had been struck. He bit his lower lip, and she gawked right back at him, intent on letting him see she wasn't in any way feeling intimidated. She believed he needed to know for certain and that he needed to see just how much she was willing to paddle through his piss and shit until she got what she wanted. Perez slowly turned around, and his knocking shoe heels faded into the distance with a relief for Heaven. "I will not be bullied or harassed," she said to herself, making sure the words rang aloud and true in her head. She had had just about enough of his nonsense, and she sought and hoped to fight back where and when she could. Sadly, the night was on the verge of being a really long one.

Chapter 6

This Man Just Won't Quit

Four months since her last episode with Perez, Heaven did away with every silly rule he stipulated for her and decided to be her own person within the office, provided it went along with the guidelines and rules every other person was following. She dumped his nasty perfume, chose what to wear when she felt like it, and wore what she wanted when she wanted.

Perez seemed to have cooled off since their last encounter, even while she sensed he was brooding and waiting for the perfect time to strike back. She didn't care, and she wasn't about to let him blindside her, so she opted to start applying for jobs once again.

For reasons she still could not make out, Michell had begun to distance herself or hardly even came around.

Sadly, the terrible jobs and tasks still had not stopped coming her way. Heaven begun to complete the tasks without complaining. She went about her tasks and smiled through them. Her relationship with the other workers also bloomed and blossomed through the months, and they managed to indulge her with respect while she made certain to reciprocate as well.

"Heaven." One of Pedro Perez's many assistants walked over to meet with Heaven while she stapled the last bit of work she just managed to finish. She glanced at her watch, noted it was past four in the afternoon and just an hour before work ends for the day, before indulging the young man. "He has really piled it on, hasn't he?" she asked in a tone that indicated she knew the man was up to no good again.

The young man shrugged and replied, "He is really mad at you, and we all can sense it."

She laughed away his claim even while she knew it was true and right. She wasn't about to quit being strong now, and without fussing about anything Perez wanted, she plucked her stapler from the desk, marched her way out of the room, and headed to the main photocopying room. She had chosen that particular photocopying room to avoid getting trapped in situations or places she would be at Perez's mercy. The day was slow, and it felt even slower when she stared down at the knee-high stack of papers she had to photocopy -- three copies each.

"That motherfucker…" She held her breath and her words with it, hoping to gain some calm and at least remain levelheaded until she could continue working.

An hour into her task and the entire office had grown

silent like a graveyard. She hurried through her business before the familiar scent of his depressing cologne hit her. "Fuck!" she bellowed. She cursed and blamed herself for not being quick enough. "Hello, Heaven." He slithered his way into the room and slowly let the door close behind him. She ignored his greeting, as she had done for weeks, and continued to work on the papers she needed to make copies of as best as she could.

"I know we got off on the wrong foot, and quite frankly, I would like to make it up to you," he whispered. She could feel his breath close to her right ear and his hand slowly settling atop her waist. Heaven spun around and shot him a side eye before returning to her work without uttering a single word. Being the defiant goat and quite pesky individual he was, he pressed forward, and this time, closed the gap between them as his chest rubbed into hers while he purred. Uncomfortable and definitely unwilling to remain in that position, Heaven tried to step to the side and away from him, but it wasn't working. He just wasn't budging.

"We are all by ourselves, and anything going on in here stays in here."

Boiling mad, tired, and getting cranky about his really despicable act, she felt something begin to poke at her from within his pants. Perez was aroused, and his hands slowly began to guide Heaven's hips, strongly refuting her effort to shove him off. "You don't need to fight it," he whispered as his horrible lips connected with her neck.

His grip got stronger the harder she pushed and

fought. Heaven sought to scream, but she wasn't about to grant him the satisfaction of acting or even looking weak. She had gone through enough in her life than to allow someone in such mold to get a hand over her. She shoved as hard as she could and refrained from giving in as he guided her toward the corner of the room. "You are feisty, and I like that in a woman," he whispered cynically.

"I am not one of those weak women who fall for your stupid antics!" she replied with verve in her voice. He was definitely not letting go, and she wondered what to do in order to get him off of her. "Get the fuck off of me!" she yelled, trying to poke him in the eye and narrowly missing. Her action only enraged him more.

Heaven wished she had come into the room with her purse; it contained her pepper spray, and he would have been far easier to repel using it. "I know you want me… I can tell from the way you've been playing hard to get." He shoved her hard into the wall and began to unbuckle his belt. His manhood was stiffened and beyond, and the look on his face terrified her badly as she struggled to get herself into a safe distance from the pervert.

"Just some minutes," he pleaded. "Just some minutes of fun, you bitch!"

Heaven groaned aloud, rammed her knee into his pelvis with all of her strength, and shoved him backward as she watched Perez crumble to the floor in agony.

He yelled and groaned, cursed at her, and swore in every language he knew, without getting back on his feet. A degree of gladness swirled through her in that moment she rammed her knee into his crotch, but she feared the worst and knew there was no going back. She had done something she would be hunted for, and she badly needed to make her way out of the office as soon as possible. Wailing in pain, his voice echoed from the distance. "Heaven! Heaven! You fucking bitch, you will pay for this!" Heaven smiled and continued to stride along the hallway with so much satisfaction and mixed emotions circling her chest. She had beaten one of her oppressors and gained her dignity back — at the expense of her job, without a doubt. The thought of that alone got tears running down her face, but it wasn't enough to cast aside her pride.

She felt happy on behalf of hundreds of other women who had been in her shoes. It was something of relief and joy for those who just couldn't stand their ground for fear of Perez making them lose their jobs or for fear of being embarrassed by the man in power. It was a proud ordeal not just for her, but also for everyone, and in that alone, she felt proud and happy.

"I wish Michell had spoken to me about him, though," she muttered to herself as she got back to her office. She figured it would have been easier had she been briefed about Perez and his offensive behavior. It didn't matter much anymore, though; she was getting kicked off this job, without a doubt. She wasn't about to grant him the satisfaction of coming back and doing so. "I won this time," she told herself. She had indeed won against her oppressor.

Chapter 7

The Ultimate Betrayal

Since Breezy had their baby girl for the day, Heaven made her way off to the bar to have some drinks before heading back to the empty walls of her apartment to cry out her eyes if need be. She was without a job, or at least once morning came that would be her fate. Her bittersweet victory needed companionship, and she figured she'd get some from the colorful bottles bearing liquids in them.

She arrived at the popular after-hours bar opposite her office and assumed her seat in her favorite corner. Michell had brought her there a couple of times to relax and converse about the day and its events. It was her first time being there without Michell, and it was pretty much odd, to say the least. Michell always had something to talk about, and hours there would get spent without them even knowing it.

"Something light, please," she ordered, citing the need to get back home without falling under the influence of alcohol. She still needed her senses intact, her mind sharp, and her thoughts in place for whatever she had to process next. With the beer bottle in her hand and her lips salivating for its quenching taste, she felt a tap on her shoulder, causing her to halt her intended acts to look to her right where the touch had come from; it was none other than Michell. Definitely unhappy with her friend and unwilling to hide it, Heaven refused to smile as she shot Michell a scowl.

"Looks like we drink without the other party now," Michell teased before ordering a drink.

Heaven wet her lips and her throat before looking back at her. "Drinking with a friend who couldn't tell me the asshole she hooked me up to work under is a pervert is a little bit hard." Michell looked at her, stared blankly at Heaven for a while, and then slowly looked away as if she wasn't ready to indulge Heaven yet. Heaven sighed, sipped from her bottle, and continued to do so in silence, albeit tormented with endless thoughts. "It isn't my fault he's a creep," Michell replied finally, without putting much importance or note to what she had said. Heaven set down her bottle to verbally tackle her friend, while she donned the most displeased expression on her face. "It isn't my fault, either, but every time I speak with you about him, you keep giving some really dismissive responses."

Michell chuckled, and stiffly so. Her action didn't seem to show she cared about how annoying or insulting her act was, and Heaven could sense something was going on.

They had been best friends for years, and it wasn't hard to spot when Michell was wound up about something or when she was actually holding something back.

Heaven turned her attention to her friend as she replaced the empty beer bottle in her hand for a full one. She wanted answers, and Michell seemed to have some she wasn't quite sharing or maybe not even willing to share. "I don't get you," Heaven muttered. "We worked there together". You helped me land this job but never mentioned or even hinted to how much of a douche this guy is."

Michell continued to sit in silence as she helped herself to gentle sips from her bottle. It felt as though she was nursing the drink, but Heaven wondered what was going through her mind and why she had decided to suddenly fall silent. It was odd, baffling, and absolutely bothersome, to say the least. "You needed a job and a better one, and I got you one. Stop bitching about it," Michell whispered grudgingly. Heaven felt her lower jaw drop and her eyes widen. Her friend had just disrespected her for reasons she couldn't quite make out yet. "Was that for me?" Heaven asked in an audacious tone. "Was that really necessary?" Michell drained her the bottle before handing it over to the bartender for a refill and granting her best friend some proper attention.

"Yeah, it was," Michell replied, flicking her hair to the side and obviously speaking with an attitude.

Heaven couldn't believe her ears, and regardless of how much she tried to think through it, she couldn't quite come up with a resolve.

"Well, it is better I inform you first before you resume work tomorrow that I will most likely be getting fired," Heaven said before looking away.

She wasn't sure what Michell's reaction was, but she could swear she heard her friend scoff. To make matters worse, Michell made no move to speak or ask any questions. She simply sipped her drink and sighed.

"Did I do something wrong?" Heaven asked to show she was bothered. "I ask because I just told you I'm losing my job, the same job we hustled to get, and here you are, drowning yourself away in a freaking beer without any concern about me!"

Michell rammed her bottle on the table, and it broke into pieces as she faced Heaven. "At least this time you get to face your mess yourself," she answered. "Perez told everyone what transpired between you and him and the news about what you did to Pedro Perez has been going around, and I honestly couldn't care less if your ass got fired tomorrow morning." Heaven's jaw felt unhinged. Her eyes widened, her brows wore a frown, and her face in totality looked lost and confused. She felt herself wanting to slap Michell into the middle of last week.

"Well, in fact, your ass is fired," Michell corrected herself.

Heaven hurriedly looked around, wondering if it was some kind of prank, or if her best friend, who was meant to grant her emotional release, was messing with her. Michell wore a smug look and continued to bear the look without an ounce of reprieve, and it forced Heaven to want to speak.

"Why are you being a bitch tonight? Considering how terrible a day I have been having, do you think this is the best time to mess around?"

Michell replied immediately. "I don't give a damn, and quite frankly I am simply watching karma mess with you on my fucking behalf."

There it was, the indication that something was wrong and that Heaven had managed to miss it all along. It was odd for Michell to keep anything from her or mock her in such a manner.

"Have I done something wrong?"

"Nope, at least not currently. But karma has found a way to bite you back in you black ass after all these years of waiting without being certain I was ever going to get satisfaction or justice for what you did back in high school," Michell explained. "I promised myself I'd chill right here, sip on some beer and feel good when you finally got what you deserved from Pedro Perez."

The vile in her voice and the tone with which she spoke caused Heaven to shift uncomfortably in her seat. It sounded as though her best friend was speaking so calmly about her debacle and was rejoicing from it as well.

"You knew he was an ass, didn't you?" Heaven asked but seemed certain of what she was talking about. "You knew pretty darn well but chose to continue acting as though you didn't when you worked in HR for some time."

"Yes, I knew, but I wasn't going to do anything about it, and certainly not for you of all people." Michell bit back. "Those days of me covering and caring for your ass are long gone!"

It didn't make an iota of sense, and regardless of how much Heaven tried to think about it, she just still could not make sense of anything. They both sat in silence, obviously stewing about their thoughts and who would speak first.

Heaven wanted her best friend to speak first and at least make it known why she was being the way she was. Michell, on the other hand, continued to snicker through the side of her mouth, and at times, heaving heavy sighs before taking more sips from her drink. "You got me this job. I just want to know why," Heaven finally said in a calm tone. It was obvious to her that she couldn't continue with the job and she definitely could not have anything to do with the office ever again.

"I did it because it was the only way to finally pay you back for what you did to me in high school," Michell said. "I trusted you, doted on you, and would go to the end of the earth with or for you, but the slightest chance you got and then you bit me in the back without even looking around."

Heaven had no idea what the subject matter was about. She struggled to relate with what her friend was talking about, but Michell seemed bent on letting her heart out. Her face donned a cynical smile, though, something that definitely indicated she was happy and pleased with the situation. "I needed you to feel what I felt in high school when shit went down and you decided to leave me alone," she explained. "It happened so many times I really had to take a stand and plan to hurt you the fuck back when the time was right."

"What…what are you even talking about?" Heaven asked in a perplexed tone. "Nothing you are saying makes any sense whatsoever."

"Do you remember the night I stood with you when you were so bent on getting Breezy for yourself?" she asked Heaven. Heaven cocked her head.

"Do you remember how I was there for you on that night and the extent we went to in bid to get the competitor off of your path?"

Heaven continued to cock her head, unsure of what to say and definitely willing to learn what exactly was going on with her friend.

"Did you ever wonder what happened after we trashed that car so you could have your time with Prince Charming?" Michell asked with a raised brow.

Heaven realized she actually didn't bother to find out. All she cared about was having Breezy, and since she managed that with Michell's help, she didn't see the need to even worry about some damaged car any longer. There was an episode after the melee, though, and she struggled recall what it was.

"Did you realize I was caught on surveillance camera in the parking lot? I was caught on camera, doing your dirty deed, just so you could be with your man and thereby I became the sole person deemed responsible for the heinous crime."

Heaven recalled the incident well enough and how badly they had busted Sonja's car. People continued to speak of the incident for about a week, and it became the talk of the town.

"IHOP security team investigated the matter and handed the surveillance footage over to the police." Michell said with a catch in her throat. "They blamed me for everything, and even while they asked if I had an accomplice in the crime, I declined to let them know about you being the master planner." Heaven could not believe her best friend had kept something of such magnitude from her for years. She had heard her friend's words, but they still didn't seem relatable, the hatred or the level of vile, which Michell had to keep inside was baffling and disturbing. "I kept this in for so long, and I continued to ponder hard on why you didn't even seem to care after everything I did for you."

Michell seemed really upset now as she rammed her fist into the wooden tabletop.

"I did care about you." Heaven tried to defend her honor, but Michell was having none of it.

"You cared? Did you say you cared?" Michell asked sarcastically.

Heaven motioned to answer but held back her words while she waited for Michell to speak some more.

"I came to you for help. I reached out to you to assist in paying off the large and fucking stupid debt they pinned on me for the stupid car that got trashed."

Michell decided to take her friend down memory lane. "What did you do?" Heaven could recall that aspect to things now. She could recall Michell reaching out to her for assistance and even hammering on how she was fucked if she didn't pay off the required damages for the car she had smashed. Remembering every inch of the past brought her discomfort and caused her to bite her lip. "Do you have any idea how long it took for me to pay off those damages?" Michell drew closer with a raised brow. "Do you have any idea what it feels like to have your best friend, the same person who was meant to be your ride-or-die and who ought to have your back, regardless of what is going on, only for her to skip off with some boy and then abandon you?" Michell was playing the guilt-trip card, and Heaven was falling hard. It was hard and bad enough that she had just lost her job, but it was troubling to find out that her best friend was targeting her as well.

"I didn't know," Heaven muttered without realizing the words had escaped her mouth.

Michell let off a loud cackle that caught the attention of everyone in the room. She ordered another beer and continued to drown herself in the intoxicating liquid, while Heaven watched on, at a loss about what to do or how to go about making the situation right with her friend who was obviously aggrieved.

"I am sorry, Michell," she finally spilled.

Michell shook her head in a nonchalant manner before replying. "You got what you fucking deserve, and I actually don't give a damn."

It hurt to hear her best friend say something of such to her. It was even more annoying and painful that Michell held it all in for that long, only to begin to scribble a plan in which Heaven was bound to fail and suffer as well.

"Do you remember your words when I came to you?" Michell asked. "Do you recall your specific words?"

"I said it wasn't my fault?" Heaven replied.

Michell jammed her bottle into the table again, but it didn't break this time around.

"No! No! No!" Michell yelled. "That wasn't what you said, and I need you to say those precise words that made me feel like a fool." The precise words were definitely more painful, and Heaven remembered them very clearly.

"I said I didn't make you do anything you didn't want to do in the first place," Heaven recited just as she had spilled the words. Michell raised her bottle and smiled. "You made me feel stupid, and now look at how stupid you look having to battle that douche called Pedro Perez through the entire damn office."

Heaven gasped in shock with the realization that her situation had been well crafted and that Michell had watched her not only struggle but suffer through her period under Pedro Perez. It was heartbreaking and draining. Her anger boiled through, and she could barely keep it away from her face. Obviously losing much more than her job on that day, Heaven realized she had just lost her friend as well, and removed herself from the table. She needed to be away from Michell and away from everything that had to do with her workplace. It felt like she had fallen down the black hole she once struggled through, taking her right back to the bottom.

Heaven walked out of the bar, feeling like she had struck rock bottom again. The overwhelming feeling of emptiness gushed and coursed through her while she dragged her feet along the pavement outside the bar and struggled to make sense of what her life held in play next. She felt empty and drained and devoid of answers. "Where do I begin from now? Where do I do next?" she asked herself.

Those were the valid questions the now jobless single mother had to ask herself.

Chapter 8

Bruised But Not Broken

Asking those questions felt hard and seemed impossible just some weeks back. In fact, they never might have popped up had she remained where she was, before forcefully paving way to attaining the new position with the help of her so-called best friend.

It felt like it had taken her ages just to walk out of the bar. Her legs weren't moving as fast as she would have wanted, and her pace was short. Her strides came slowly, and her eyes bore nothing but regrets. The reality still felt as if it eluded her for a moment. The truth behind what had just befallen her still didn't seem real.

Something had gone terribly wrong for Heaven, and she wondered when it would really dawn on her or when she was finally going to see it for what it was. Her chest thudded hard and wouldn't stop. Her eyes watered desperately, and her lips began to tremble, but no drop of tears made its way down her cheeks, and no ounce of pain trickled down her spine just yet. Her response to the current situation was odd, and she wondered what others in her shoes would naturally do.

Would they cry? Would they get angry? Would they blame someone else? These questions loomed through her mind, but she found no reasoning behind any. None seemed fit for her to follow, and she wasn't even sure of what she felt in that moment. Some feet away from the law firm, eyes fixated on the huge doors she had often walked into proudly and with warmth in her heart before she started working for Pedro Perez, floods of regrets began to well inside her. Yet Heaven refused to cry…yet. She refused to let down or through any form of tears yet, until she was certain of what was going on with her.

The endless nights she spent trying to please her law firm, the days used up while she attempted to give her best, and the breaks she never even had the opportunity to take because she didn't want to give anyone any reason at all to attack her competence, all seemed like a waste of time now. The most painful aspect to it all was devoting time meant to be spent with her daughter to be able to meet with the office demands. "Crazy world," she whispered without actually thinking or assuming the need to take responsibility for her actions just yet.

Her world was crazy, her life was maddening, and above all, her night was souring fast. She waddled through the street before her, empty in mind and unsure of what would happen next. There were endless possibilities of how things could have gone wrong for her at her workplace, but

Heaven never assumed it was ever going to have anything to do with her best friend orchestrating it.

The betrayal, the anguish that came with getting the job in the first place, coupled with the eventual loss of the job accompanied her through the night as she walked away with no aim and no destination in mind. The thought of returning home barely crossed her mind, or at least it didn't linger there yet. She didn't want to go back there for reasons that rang aloud in her head continuously.

"I left home as an employed woman," she whispered to herself as she recounted the reality of old and that of new now facing her. "Now, I have to go back as an unemployed woman."

Her heart finally broke, and Heaven fell on her knees. She could swear both knees almost shattered as she rammed them into the earth and tilted her head forward. Her eyes overflowed with water, and her lips finally succumbed to the order of pain coursing through her very soul. She wept profusely and wailed, right there in the middle of the street, without holding back. The end was upon her, and she didn't know how best to go about it. "How is this even possible?" was the final question on her lips. It was surreal, but it had happened, and she was witnessing it without doubt.

At home, Heaven toyed with her phone and barely noted the time or how it had swept past her. All she could focus her mind on was the failure and loss and everything else that was bound to come with it. She scrolled through her timeline and checked her messages to see if there was anything new, but nothing.

"Crazy world," she noted to herself.

Even her best friend didn't seem to care about the fact she had just lost her job and in no small part because she had been the orchestrator. Slowly, Heaven tilted her head backward on her couch to see the wall clock and hear it chime to announce the stroke of midnight. She had arrived home two hours prior, and sleep eluded her. It helped that Breezy had decided to take care of their daughter for the night and with the arrangement that he would drop her off at Heaven's mother's place should things become too hectic for him to handle. It would grant her time alone, or at least the moment to wallow in her shame and any form of pity she could muster.

The fact her mother was bound to grow concerned and ask questions when she went to pick her daughter the following day made things feel even worse. It made her stomach sink and her throat fill with painful and bitter regrets.

"Why me?" she asked before her phone beeped and an email message came through.

Unsure of what it was, but with her heart wishing there was some way out of the mess she had gotten herself into, she yanked the phone off of the couch, scrolled through, and hoped to see something positive. The moment her eyes fell on the phone screen, they widened and she let off a loud gasp. *This cannot be true.*

The information definitely didn't tally with everything that had happened, but it seemed to suggest the possibility of being granted a second chance. Such chances were rare and almost impossible in cases such as hers, and while she didn't know who had gone the mile on her behalf, or who could have done something so daring, she felt super excited and read the message again and again.

"Dear Ms. Davis,

The Managing Partners would like to have a meeting with you at 10:00 a.m. this Friday at the law firm. Kindly bear in mind that in light of recent events, you are still entitled to a full investigation and still remain a member of our staff unless stated otherwise."

She jumped off her couch, read the message aloud, and heard herself begin to pant uncontrollably before finally deciding it was best she calmed her nerves. "I can still beat this! I can still beat this!" she shouted with joy while she stomped her feet.

Heaven decided she would build her defense in the best way possible, hurrying over to her desk to begin scribbling points and notions she hoped to make when she got back to the office on Friday Second chances were rare, but it felt like she had been granted one by forces unknown. She did her job well and must have garnered some proper appreciation from other managers, however there was still the problem of Pedro Perez.

They must be gathering a committee to look into the matters at hand, she thought, delighted. *Justice will be served, and this will be sorted.* It was the only conclusion she could come to, considering she had not done anything wrong until Perez forced her hand into harming him. *If they need proof, I have it.*

Through the darkened clouds that lay ahead of her before, Heaven seemed to see a silver lining, and in that, she hoped to ride her luck until something good came out of it. She wasn't one to shy away from standing up for herself, especially in a case or in a time like this. She felt pumped up, filled with energy and verve, and absolutely ready to tear through anything else in her path.

All you have to do is defend yourself, she thought. *You were wronged, and in time they will realize what form of sexual predator Pedro Perez truly is.*

Heaven figured it shouldn't be hard to tender her case and to make it very much believable, considering how many more ladies had suffered in his hands and how many more they could certainly prevent and protect from meeting similar fate.

"Whoa! Thank you, Jesus!" she screamed in joy and with some form of relief at the possibility of being vindicated. The feeling was beyond priceless; it was pretty much intoxicating and nerve jolting. She picked up her pen, opened her notepad, and began to scribble as fast as possible.

Chapter 9

Hurt and Devastation

Friday

The early hours of the morning came with a refreshing feeling. It didn't just come sooner than Heaven had expected it to, but it felt absolutely soothing, to say the least. There were stings of nervousness troubling her to some degree, but Heaven had convinced herself not to get trampled upon by any of it. In fact, she felt she was about as ready as any successful and cocky lawyer would be when they were about to walk into the court to win a case they just could not lose.

The worst they would do is suspend me for being physical. She grinned as she held open the front door and stepped into the lobby.

Everyone and everything seemed to stop for a moment, as eyes fixated on her and people began to leer. The sight was uncomfortable, but she soaked them all in, hoping their voices of congratulations would be as adoring just in the same way as their drowning gazes threatened to unsettle her.

"You got this, girl." She encouraged herself as she began her slow and tentative walk through the bodies of onlookers. Their gazes refused to tear off of her until she stepped into the elevator. Heaven let off a loud sigh in relief and crouched to her knees as she took a moment to get some much-needed air. She couldn't believe she survived walking through such a massive crowd, one that she didn't know what they had in their heads or running through their minds. *Are they worried about me?* she asked herself. *Did they look worried about me?* She couldn't quite tell which it was, but she wasn't about to allow herself to crumble now. She wasn't about to watch herself succumb to crumbling under a fate she wasn't even sure or convicted for just yet. She prepared to fight, and that was exactly what she hoped to do. It even reflected in her dressing for the morning.

Heaven had chosen her classic "tough character" look. She donned no makeup, decided to put on pants instead of a skirt, and even did away with her purse or any form of extra attachment as she walked into the building that morning. Thankfully, Breezy had still not called to complain about their daughter, and she figured he could take care of her much longer than planned.

"Mama has some butts to kick," she had muttered to herself after checking her phone and seeing no missed calls or messages from her daughter's father.

The elevator doors chimed and slowly opened, and the last person on earth she ever imagined she'd be looking at stepped right to the door. His face bore the most irritating smirk, and his smug expression threatened to cause her to puke. He grinned, seemed to take his time before stepping into the elevator, even while Heaven wished he had taken another one. The air between them suddenly thinned and became almost unbearable. She cringed on the inside and wished she had been some minutes late; after all, it was just nine, and her meeting was slated for ten.

Pedro Perez. The words bounced around her mind and came with a really troubling amount of feeling.

She turned to the wall, hoping to consume herself and her presence with her own reflection from the shiny surface. Unfortunately, it wasn't hard to see the annoying smirking face glaring right back at her from the reflection. He was there to torment her, and she wouldn't put it past him to have found out about her arrival and bid the perfect moment to get into the elevator with her. "Why?" she asked without directing the vague question at him. She wished she could get an apt response, but the chances of that were bound to be slim. She was determined not to cry or get angry, regardless of the circumstances. The plan felt like one that would fall off the hinges soon, especially if she remained within those walls with the man longer than she intended to.

"Today is a big day for us both, isn't it?" he asked in a cocky tone. "You are trying to defend your honor, while I am bound to do the same."

He didn't sound bothered, and by hearing the cockiness in his tone, she could very well swear he was being absolutely confident about his chances. It made Heaven worry, and it made her uncomfortable. He bore no remorse in his tone, and he definitely didn't have any on his face as he continued to smirk at her.

She shook her head, turned back to look at him and finally said the only word she could muster, "Why?"

Perez shrugged his shoulders, smirked right back, and replied, "Why not?" It was and would be the only meaningful conversation they would have before the elevator doors opened to allow her exit again. Heaven rushed out, almost as if she had been camped with a swarm of bees, taking to her heels and headed for the conference room where the meeting was bound to happen. On the other hand and in quite majestic manner, Perez tailed her, smiling and whistling without an ounce of worry in the world.

I cannot lose against that jerk! Heaven warned herself. The risks were just too great, and the rewards were equally heightened for her to miss out on. The fears of having to search for a new job out there kept her will and resolve to win even higher as she settled herself into an empty seat and tilted her head to pray, or at least do away with the negative energy slowly surrounding her.

Perez took his time while he traipsed the floor outside the conference room. The transparent glass permitted Heaven ample opportunity to look at her abuser. With each sight she caught of him, she felt something fuel even more inside of her. Her emotions threatened to get the better of her, and while she struggled to contain them, Perez wasn't doing anything to help matters instead. Time trickled by and painfully so. Breezy had still not reached out, and Heaven took that as a sign that things were going well. She glanced through her notes once again, read them in her head in hopes nobody was listening, and structured them into the most articulate defense she had ever managed to do, and all felt perfect. Well, all felt perfect until "she" walked in.

Heaven's lower jaw dropped at the sight of her supposed best friend. There had been no indication that Michell had any reason to be in the room. In fact, Heaven could not even relate with or even come to an understanding as to why her best friend, who had stabbed her in the back for months out of vengeance, was now at her meeting.

They greeted each other with silence, and their stanch gazes were enough to show there was no love lost between the duo. Michell assumed the seat next to Heaven for reasons unknown to the latter. Yet, Heaven wasn't about to allow something of such nature topple her. She wasn't there for Michell, and she definitely was not there for anyone but herself.

Perez finally returned to the room, and Heaven watched him flank her to the left. They were seated on each side of her, sandwiching her in the middle in what felt too much like a coincidence. They were smirking too, and irritatingly so. The need to keep her cool proceeded over others, and that was exactly what she opted to do.

You can win. Heaven thought to herself. *Babe, you got this!*

She probably wouldn't have mentioned it, but a part of her was feeling overwhelmed, and whatever confidence she had ridden on through the lobby walk and into the elevator was now desperately shaky. It felt as though she was struggling to even exist within herself, and while she sat there, between two people she didn't want anything to do with in that moment, breathing became harder.

Thankfully, the managing partners soon arrived, and they seemed eager to get things sorted and sealed. They assumed their seats around the rectangular meeting table and the lead managing partner was present. It was surprising, considering few people know him personally, aside from the information about the prominent mole hanging on his chin, which made it easy to spot the man anywhere.

Heaven took some measure of comfort and relief in the fact the Perez was present; it came with the sense that to a good extent something was about to go down.

"Ms. Davis the man called out, signaling for her to get on her feet.

Heaven cleared her throat while his assistants took their positions to record the meeting. The lead managing partner narrated what she had sent to them in defense of her actions and what had transpired over the course of her work months under Pedro Perez.

The lead managing partner of the law firm raised his right hand and silenced his assistant. "I want to listen to the real thing as it happened and how this young lady managed to handle the entire process." Heaven couldn't quite believe her ears. She looked at Michell, and in that period, wanted to shame her friend for their previous conversation the night before. It was time for Heaven to clear herself of any form of wrongdoing, and maybe even seek some degree of compensation. She had researched well enough on the issue of abuse in workplaces, especially one where there was abuse of power in the light of sexual components (months prior when she first discovered the possibility that she was being sexually harassed).

In most cases, there was compensation being made, and often-in monetary terms.

"Good morning, everyone, and I am pleased and honored to be granted this opportunity to air my grievances and defend myself against what I believe to be injustice," Heaven began. She would spend the next half hour spelling out everything she suffered and even managed to back them up with chats and conversations that she exchanged with Pedro Perez through the course of the abuse. She tendered her cell phone and made sure every single message in which she corresponded with the man was read and noted. She felt her case was solid and believed in justice prevailing as she finally returned to her seat.

"If I may reiterate your points, Ms. Davis." The lead managing partner cleared his throat. "Mr. Pedro Perez instigated a lot of sexual favors from you and even went as far as harassing you inside the law firm?"

"That is correct," Heaven replied without being

scared one bit of where she was and all she had said. She was asked to sit, and Perez was called forward.

"Thank you," he said with a grin while he unbuttoned his suit coat. "While I have listened to every blasphemous information this young lady has uttered, I can assure you that nothing of what she laid into evidence is true."

Heaven gasped, shocked by the man's bold denial and the manner in which he went about it. He didn't seem to care, either, and while she listened on, it became clear just how manipulative the man she was dealing with was. His words were stinging lies, and the precision with which he dropped them was very easy to believe.

"I never made a move or even attempted to harass Ms. Davis," he claimed. "I wasn't even supposed to hire her in the first place."

Something about that latter sentence and statement caused the hairs on the back of her neck to stand. They caused her to cringe inside and grope the arms of her chair before slowly turning her gaze to her best friend. Michell wasn't looking her way, and it was evident that something was going on.

Michell seemed awfully relaxed and calm as could be too. Heaven shifted in distress in her seat, listened to Perez narrate the story on how he wasn't supposed to hire Heaven and how he had intended to pick someone else, but the list he had to work with had been deliberately streamlined. "She was cunning and callous right from the start, and she deliberately went on to trim the applicant pool by discarding those who had better resumes than hers and with more work experience, while she left behind those less qualified for the job," he explained in detail and with so much commitment to it as well. Heaven felt the world sneak off from underneath her feet, and the longer she tried to think about it, the more disturbed she was. There was only one way she could have been made out, and that was through the help of her perceived best friend.

I should have known. Heaven lowered her head in shame. It wasn't bad enough that her friend had put her into such a mess; she was now there to add more salt to her wound at the expense of simply making a point and validating her ego. It was oddly surprising, considering she had never seen or even assumed Michell in such light before.

"This is the same person crying foul before you all to ruin my reputation in this office and to cast me off as an inconsiderate sexual pervert, which I am not!"

Pedro Perez ended his statement and returned to his seat. He was winning, and very much so.

Heaven swallowed hard and reached for her phone. "But I have messages showing he was harassing me," she said, hoping she would some way actually get the justice she deserved. "I have everything right here, and you saw it."

Perez scoffed. "I can bet the messages aren't mine. She does not even have my contact information." She couldn't believe her ears, but he was aiming at something, and she was walking right into it. Corroborating the fact was that she didn't have his contact information when they compared their phones. The sneaky man, so experienced in covering his steps, had been conversing with her using a different phone, most likely a burner, for that matter.

This is bad. Heaven knew. Her only hope to make things right and be in her favor would be for Michell to disclaim everything about how they manipulated the hiring process until she got the job. They had done it together, and the culpability that they would both have to dance to the tune of things was high, but Michell didn't seem at all worried as she stood to her feet.

"I know my relationship with the defendant will make things look really bad, but I assure you about having nothing to do with any of this," she stated. "I also come bearing gifts to attest to certain shredded documents in form of applicant's resumes which the accused asked me to dispose of on her behalf."

Heaven clamped her hands over her face and wished the earth beneath would swallow her whole. With her best friend's testimony against her, there was no going back, and there would or could be no winning either. She watched them slowly pile up the shredded resumes, which she assumed were long gone, before placing them atop the table in testament and verification of everything that was being said.

Whatever proof she had on her cell phone, defense she hoped to use and the plan she had concocted through the night immediately went flying out the window.

"Is there anything you would like to add to any of these, Ms. Davis?" the lead managing partner asked. Heaven couldn't bear to look up at him. She was overwhelmed and had lost. Everything had turned upside down from the moment Michell walked into that room. The reason for her presence was now known.

"If you have nothing to defend yourself by and quite obviously you cannot or shouldn't." The lead managing partner took a lengthy sigh. "You are terminated, effective immediately. All of your personal items will be boxed and delivered to you by courier within 48-business hours. You will be escorted from the premises."

It had been made official; she lost her job. The thought was surreal, but so was the occurrence. This time around, there was more shame attached to it. As she helped herself up from her seat, she could have sworn she heard her best friend snicker. It wasn't loud, but it did not have to be loud for her to know she had been screwed over.

Heaven exited the room with law firm security in tow with her dignity dragged along the floor. The elevator seemed farther from her the closer she got to it.

The more she thought of everything that had happened in the conference room, the more convinced she was that things were never going to go well for her. *She betrayed me* were the words she could taste at the tip of her tongue. There was no other way to say it, but her friend deceived her, and it hurt like hell. "Heaven," Michell called out just as Heaven stepped into the elevator. Heaven looked away and cast her gaze to the ground without any response.

"Why?" she finally asked. "Was getting your revenge not enough a week ago? Considering you know how much I have to lose with this job gone, what would make you stand behind Pedro Perez and not me?" Michell replied, "It was the only way I would get promoted, and more so, you still didn't suffer as much as I wanted you to." The ride in the elevator became even more uncomfortable until the doors opened. Michell stepped out first and waved mockingly before Heaven followed suit and watched her friend disappear from sight. The gawking personalities gathered in the lobby continued to look at her in a nerve-racking manner until she finally got outside of the building.

She threw up on the sidewalk and wiped her mouth clean with her tissue.

It was the end of the road for her there, and no sooner had she stepped forward and planned to head home did Breezy's call come through.

"Hey! I had to drop the little princess off at your mom's," he said. "Gotta run!"

The call came to an end, and Heaven slid her phone back into her pocket. She had to be at her mother's; she had to be with the two most important females in her life who couldn't and wouldn't betray or hurt her.

Thoughts of what Michell had done would haunt her until she got to her mother's place. The years they spent together had been washed down the drain in a manner she had never seen coming.

She wished she had apologized to her friend the week before, but it was of no use doing so when her so-called friend couldn't even set things right between them after so many years had passed.

Chapter 10
Another Opportunity Came Knocking

"In my opinion, the friendship wasn't worth it," her mother said while she did the dishes. Heaven barely listened to her mom while she glanced into the beautiful and innocent eyes of her daughter. "Friends don't do that to each other, and in my opinion, that job wasn't on the verge of lasting either," her mother continued before returning with a clean mug that she set on the table before her daughter.

It sounded like one of those classic moments where she got lectured really hard and really well on the importance of actually going through due processes and not cutting corners.

"Something good is around the corner, and you don't have to wallow in pity or pain for much longer," her mother said in positivity.

She cocked her head and decided to believe in the positive words while she gave Hilly some water. No sooner had she taken her mind off things did her cell phone ring.

"Oh my God!" Heaven exclaimed, almost causing her mother to drop a saucer in her hand. "What?"

"One of the many applications I completed during my last job just came through," she replied. She turned away immediately to call the phone number included with the message. She could feel herself sweating profusely. The line connected, and she spoke with the responder for a while before returning into the kitchen with a rather gloomy appearance. "They cancelled the appointment," she said to her mother.

It was bizarre and baffling, but it was what the lady on the other end of the line had told her and with some apologies. She felt her mood get dragged down to earth and plummet further beneath as she bent her head into the table to weep. She would cry her eyes out for the next hour without accepting any form of consolation from her mother.

Her major regrets bordered around allowing herself to indulge in such fraudulent job-attaining schemes or even allowing Michell to lead her through the entire process. She was back to square one, where she had nothing to offer herself, her daughter, or even her mother. Heaven's mother, ever so understanding, patted her daughter on the back while she spoke warm and kind words to her distraught daughter. "We should get out of your way for now," her mother finally said, before picking up Hilly and heading to the spare room to play with her granddaughter.

The next week would go by with nothing interesting happening. Endless streams of frustration and an innate feeling of pain that just could not be quenched would characterize each day.

Two Weeks Later

Like a charm and as if things were beginning to look up for her again, Heaven got called in for an interview in Rockville, Maryland. The details of the interview had clearly stated the role, but she wasn't entirely sure of what it would entail until she arrived at the office, nervous and somewhat jittery.

The line of people before her waiting to get interviewed was lengthy, and it was slowly beginning to turn her interest off as well. Her turn finally approached, and she stepped into the interview to the sight of a burly man with a stern gaze and an extended arm inviting her to take her seat. "I will be direct, and I need you to be precise as well," he said. "My name is Alexander Knot, and you may refer to me only as Alexander, and not Alex or Knot."

She nodded her head and replied, "Yes, sir."

The office definitely looked big, and the cubicles she managed to see before being asked into the office where the actual interview was being conducted indicated they had lots of staff working on every floor within the building. "What you are being interviewed for is a position for a live answering machine service which is primarily what we do here," the man explained. "How good are your communication skills, how well are you with following orders, and if you got the job, how soon can you begin?"

A million and one things were running through her

mind in that moment.

The location was far from where she lived, and getting to work would demand taking the bus, which wasn't going to be comfortable. On the other hand, she needed the job and the pay, which was bound to come with it. There were bills to pay, and Breezy still had not managed to sort himself out financially, much less of being able to rely on him.

Fuck! Heaven thought to herself before straightening her sitting posture and leaning forward to answer the man. Her response seemed to delight the man from the onset, and while she spoke, he listened attentively.

"I need you to start tomorrow," the man said as soon as she had gotten through her pitch. "I need you to begin work here tomorrow morning and with no excuses if you plan to accept the job offer." It wasn't hard to tell he wasn't one to bend for others, even though he didn't come off as rude in any way.

"What exactly would my job be?" she asked, hoping to get enough clarification before plunging herself into it.

"You will be tasked with receiving calls and messages on behalf of reputable doctors' offices," Alexander replied. "Is this going to be a problem for you?"

Heaven had no response other than a resounding "No." She watched Alexander reach underneath the table, take out a large book, and place it before her. "That's the company manual, which you will need to refer to over the next few weeks in order to learn your job." The thick book, definitely bulkier than anything she had successfully read when she was in school, seemed like cause for concern.

"I take details seriously, Miss Davis. I need you to have the contents of this book digested and in your memory before you start work tomorrow," he warned. It seemed unbelievable, but he was being serious, and she had nothing but a sharp nod to give before exiting his office. On the bus back home, Heaven helped herself to the first few pages of the book. It was boring as hell, draining, and bore no firm interest for her, regardless of how much she read it or how far she tried to cover.

"This is the way forward," she sang to herself while the bus ride seemed like it was forever. It became apparent that the job wasn't as stressful as she assumed it would be. The manual was lifesaving and educative, and above all, had been written and authored by Alexander Knot himself. "You have got to be kidding me," she mumbled upon seeing his name on the back of the book.

She finally arrived at her stop and headed to Hilly's day care. Walking into the complex, expecting to get her child, Heaven failed to see any traces of Hilly amid the four kids left to get picked by their parents. Immediately and with worry welling up inside of her, she rushed to the front desk to speak with the receptionist in charge.

"Hello," she greeted the woman calmly while she was beginning to freak out on the inside. The lady at the reception replied without allowing Heaven speak. "Breezy came to pick her as you permitted."

Heaven looked at the lady with extreme irritation, before taking a good look at the permission form she had signed when she dropped her daughter off that morning.

"We wouldn't hand over children unless there is a signed agreement from the parent dropping them off." She exhaled in relief and called Breezy's phone immediately. He confirmed he had Hilly and laid Heaven's mind to rest. Heaven thanked the receptionist and hurried back home where her daughter and her daughter's father were having a wonderful time together. Seeing him willing to assist was a heartwarming sight, but his demons remained, and that in itself was bound to continue causing issues between them.

"Babe, how was the job interview?" he asked from where he was playing with Hilly. Heaven slipped off her dress and tossed it into the laundry bin before replying. "It went well, but I feel my new boss might be a nut job." She could hear Breezy laugh hard.

"Been there, done that!"

She refused to respond to his words and decided to help herself to a relieving shower before going back out to cook dinner and play with her daughter.

The day was tiring already and was only going to get worse if she continued on an empty stomach with a really sticky body.

It would take her some time, but she finally got through the tasks and collapsed in a heap on the couch while Breezy brought over their daughter.

"Did she give you trouble?" Heaven asked.

Breezy shook his head. "She was a delight as usual, and I feel me and her are really hitting it off now."

Hilly was easy to handle once she was comfortable with you. More so, Breezy had a way with her, and he did an excellent job in ways those at the day care center couldn't even dream of doing. He doted on his baby girl, and Heaven couldn't quite appreciate him enough for it. His demons were just too much for her to handle, and hence the separation still lasting between them. "So, how do you plan on navigating the entire ordeal?" he asked thoughtfully.

"It isn't going to be an easy ride shuffling Hilly and your new job. So what's your plan?"

"I really don't know," she answered honestly.

"How about I drop you off on days I sleep over like today, and I can help take Hilly to day care too?" he asked. "This way, you don't have much to worry about, and we can actually make things work." Hearing him use the word "we" brought butterflies to her stomach, but she soon nudged the feeling away. She agreed with his plan and thanked him for even bringing it up. It wouldn't entirely erase her problems, but it would at least help her solve some of them. More so, it would relieve the stress on Hilly, who was the innocent sufferer in the entire thing.

"Looks like everything is in order, then." He chuckled.

She smiled back at him, knowing their night was bound to be fun. She would put her baby girl to bed sooner than later and have the remaining night for herself and

Breezy.

Heaven arrived at work as expected and early too. Surprisingly, Alexander stood by the gate, watching everyone go by and personally stamping their time cards as they did so. He was a hands-on kind of person, without a doubt, and she watched him ask a number of them questions before they stepped in.

She drew closer, holding her manual tightly to her chest and hoping the man wouldn't have anything to say to her. His eyes saw everything as he pulled a lady over for wearing inappropriate colored shoes. "You know the rules," he said before holding his hand in the direction of the gate.

The manual he had given Heaven clearly stated the need for uniform shoes and clothing. They were mandated to have on black shoes at all times, with words clearly stating how they weren't in there for fashion.

"Good morning, Miss Davis. Kindly wait in my office for a quick test before being granted entrance into the main building."

She could not believe her ears, but he was serious. She wasn't the only one, as evident by the five other people waiting for him in his office. "I learned he is nuts," a guy said while he brushed his hair back with his hands. "My brother has worked for him for four years, and he has never been late or even missed a day at work. He didn't take a day off when his father passed away last year."

Heaven heard her heartbeat and felt her soul worry about her new boss before she heard him open the door and prompt everyone into order. He said nothing and approached his desk before handing out sheets with names and details of the test taker already printed on each one they were being given.

"I need the answers in the next five minutes," he said before resting in his chair and watching the applicants. The six of them looked at each other, obviously confused and unsure of how to express their worries about their new boss. Heaven proceeded to finish the test and he graded her right there and then.

"Your penmanship needs work, but you had an eight, which isn't excellent but isn't bad, either," he said as he handed her test back to her. "I need a ten next time, and that can only happen if you finish reading the entire manual I gave to you."

He graded the others. Two people got below seven, which according to Alexander was unacceptable.

"You both are dismissed," he said there and then and without an ounce of pity or emotion on his face. The words left the strangest expression on Heaven's face, as it did those of the men she was standing with. It was unbelievable and absolutely confusing too.

"I have rules made, and I expect them to be followed," he said. "What are we if we cannot abide by simple rules? I cannot work with unintelligent beings unwilling to learn and unwilling to do what is right."

Heaven listened attentively, hoping she wasn't going to miss anything he said or forget anything he was trying to teach her. They marched out of the office and headed over to the main area, taking notes one at a time and constantly being corrected by Alexander every step of the way. The entire day would be spent learning the basics of working at a live answering service call center before Heaven finally go assigned a cubicle, south of Alexander's office.

"You know the rules. You know what to do and what not to do," he stated before turning around. "I don't pay you to stand in a spot! Get to work immediately!"

Heaven rushed over to her cubicle, settled into it, and began to prepare herself for the first call she would receive. Without taking long, the first phone call came through. She steadied herself in mind and body to receive it. Thankfully, Heaven resolved the caller's situation fast and promptly so.

"Nicely done." Alexander's voice came from behind. "Your average handling time should be good by the end of the day."

His voice startled her, no doubt, and the fact he had a stopwatch in hand, timing her call length and even monitoring her so-called Average Handling Time (AHT) was baffling. She had no idea he was behind her, and her nerves continued to stiffen until he walked away, presumably to torment the next guys. "What the fuck?" She gasped and shook her head. She was definitely dealing with a crazy ass, and she already couldn't wait to get a different job. By the end of the day, all she'd have to talk about with her colleagues was how their new boss creeped them the hell out. He timed calls, snuck up on unsuspecting workers, and even reprimanded them for their eating habits when they were on breaks. A complete dick.

"I am not sure I'll make it past a month here," a guy by the name Tony said as they walked toward the bus later in the evening. He looked at Heaven, shot her a smile, and approached her without taking note of his bus leaving. He'd missed his bus.

"Are you from around here?" he asked.

She shook her head. "I live pretty far away."

"Would you like to hang out some time?"' he asked, coming off as jumpy.

She shook her head and replied, "Thanks for the offer, but I am engaged in various activities for now."

Normally, Heaven would have agreed, or at least she would have if Michell were by her side. She had not gone on a date for a while, and Breezy wasn't being the man in her life in ways she wanted.

There was another hindering factor why she wasn't interested in meeting men just yet—her shape.

Spending those weeks at home doing nothing had not done her any positive service.

Instead, she added weight and slowly felt as though she was losing her perfect body. Granted, the slender long legs remained, but she wanted herself in top shape before she would attempt to go out with anyone.

Get your chubby ass back in the gym, then! she thought

before boarding her bus home.

During the bus ride, Heaven would peruse the contents of her manual over and over and again until she was satisfied. She wasn't about to leave anything to chance with Alexander and his overbearing personality.

"Is this the best I can get?" she asked herself as she neared her stopping point.

Spotting Breezy's car in the parking lot was evidence he was around. She'd have preferred he didn't have to be around all the time, but she had no choice for now. He was helping out, and that was what she needed until things finally got stable. She wasn't where she wanted to be, in shape and in regard to her job just yet.

"Guess who's home!" she chimed from the doorstep before pulling open the storm door and walking into her living room. Breezy had made a mess of things while trying to entertain their daughter. Heaven sighed in a show of tiredness before picking up her daughter and planting warm kisses on her cheeks.

"I missed you, honey," she whispered. It was a fitting end to an otherwise crazy day at work, spending it with her daughter while she had help on the side.

"How was work today?" Breezy asked. Hoping she didn't have to recall anything that occurred during the day, she cocked her head and smiled teasingly before carrying Hilly away.

Chapter 11
Major Relationship Issues

Everything about working in her new office came with some measure of stress. Oftentimes, Heaven felt like she was walking on eggshells; above all, it wasn't getting any easier combining her role as a mother with her new job. Hilly was a priority, and one she couldn't ignore. Getting her from day care was becoming even more difficult because Breezy's nonchalant nature had begun to worsen by the day.

On her day off, Heaven decided to make it count for her. She had spent so much time indulged in the office and other people's business that she was slowly beginning to lose track of the time she carved out just for herself. It needed to end, or at least she sought ways to try and balance things out. That was what brought the idea of hitting the gym.

Aside from the fact she was losing her somewhat perfect shape and slowly getting dragged into gaining chunks of fat she didn't want or need, there was the feeling she got when people appreciated her looks and her physique.

For Heaven, attention wasn't hard to come by; regardless of how much she didn't seek or go searching for it, it would always come. In her new workplace, in the absence of her supervisor, other workers hit on her and sent the most alluring and wonderful words as well as signals. Her perfect butt brought her immense stares, and her charming smile and beauty brought her favors without even needing to ask for them. That in itself made things easier for her at work and ensured she kept conscious of her body and how much she was falling off the fitness wagon.

"Eight is the shape to be," she would remind herself when temptations in form of unhealthy meals came her way. Yet, it wasn't as easy as she expected it to be.

In fact, with her new job, she was more inclined to eat unhealthily and delve into food items she wouldn't normally have, plus the job was sedentary in nature.

Hence, the need for gym and the need to maintain her state of mind came to be.

For Heaven, hitting the gym wasn't entirely or solely about ensuring her body would be in shape, but as a means to trim her mind and ensure it remains in focus.

When she had goals or a new goal to work through or sort out, she would hit the gym and ensure her mind found ways to delve into everything on her mind.

It was what drove her out of her house that Saturday.

Armed with her gym bag and Hilly by her side, Heaven headed for the gym in Breezy's truck, which he had agreed to leave behind for her the night before to use.

"Looks like it is just you and Mama for today." Heaven giggled as she looked at her curly-head baby girl. She made a brief stop by McDonalds to get Hilly her favorite meal—chicken nuggets, apple slices, and apple juice. It often kept her calm through the entire process of being in the gym day care. Hilly would smile during her meals, flushing red in the face at her mother and sending the warm assurance of love and admiration toward Heaven. The warm smile was reassuring, and it would be the first time she was taking Hilly to the gym with her. Since she learned they had a very good day care section at the gym, it made working out convenient and very comfortable. For one, she could drop by and check in on her daughter during breaks and easily pick her up on her way home.

Over the past three weeks, Heaven had made herself a regular at the gym not too far off from her house. It was comfortable and well equipped, with not too many people roaming the place, and an atmosphere that was welcoming. It was the same way on that day after dropping Hilly off and walking to her workout station.

Eyes trailed her on that particular morning, no doubt, and Heaven did what she knew how to do best—soak it all in.

Summer is coming, she reminded herself as she did some light stretches. She had to keep fit and get back her bikini body. She wasn't about to remain at home, waiting for Breezy to get his shit together. She could get any man she wanted, and judging by the endless smiles and winks she was getting on that particular morning, she was sure her shape was slowly gaining its form again. "Time to get busy," she muttered, doing her final stretch before taking steps forward toward the aerobics section.

The day drifted by, but Heaven remained keen on getting her tasks done before heading back home. With beads of sweat trickling down her face, her entire body was drenched. With several whistles and acknowledgment from men around her, she felt really good about her gym session that day. In fact, she felt wonderful and was spurred on to last longer than usual. Heaven was indeed "feeling herself". She took a break to check on her daughter and ensured she got fed properly. Her attention and focus fell to her workouts majorly until she noticed "them" again, just as she had done some evenings back and some time before then when she came for her workout sessions.

She looked away momentarily, hoping to avoid "them," but it was harder than she had thought or even assumed it would be.

They stared at her and trailed her every move. Those familiar eyes she had caught staring at her and sneaking peeks at her for some time now belonged to a young lady whose attention she now knew she had captured.

Their paths had never crossed per se, but she couldn't help but notice the girl constantly staring at her during her workout sessions. The interest was uncanny, to say the least.

For some reason, it only spurred Heaven on, and it would drive her desire to return to the gym and even intensify her workouts without realizing it. It was this way on one particular evening after she had left work and decided to bring Hilly with her to the gym.

Things weren't different from other times, and the girl still remained in her favored spot, eyeing Heaven and passing off thin smiles her way intermittently. Oddly, Heaven got used to men being the ones to compliment and appreciate her appearance and presence in the gym, but never a girl like her.

This particular evening, she donned her super cute pink workout gear with a fresh pair of Nikes. She wasn't sure what she had donned them for, but for weeks she had gained the interest of the other girl, and it seemed rather interesting to have her watch Heaven through her entire workout sessions. In fact, Heaven seemed to be feeding off of it.

Heaven turned to look at her admirer, but the girl wasn't seated on her bench anymore. A little bit disappointed, she sighed and turned away, only to almost lose her breath as she saw the girl stand before her with a smile.

"Oh God! You almost scared me." Heaven cackled while she held her chest tightly.

The girl waved and apologized before speaking in a subtle and yet alluring tone. "I am so sorry I startled you, but I was wondering if you needed help in lifting that."

Heaven looked at her and then over to the dumbbell before her. "Oh, that? Thanks a lot, but I got it," she replied in the fakest high-pitched voice she could muster. "What's your name?" She wondered if she had been too forward, but she felt compelled to ask and put a name to the face always staring at her.

"Jazz," the girl replied sweetly.

Heaven took the moment to look at the girl up close and personal. There was no doubt about her beauty, and she wasn't typical feminine-looking woman, either.

She bore the appearance of one of the best-looking athletic women one could ever see. While Heaven continued to leer at her, things were undoubtedly on the verge of becoming awkward. Jazz's body was mesmerizing beyond doubt. She was tall, caramel skinned, and with short, curly natural black hair. Her slim and sexy muscular build got Heaven salivating without realizing it, and her entire frame was beyond cute as Heaven found herself barely blinking the entire time through. Heaven, for a fact, had always found herself being attracted to people with strong muscular arms. She loved the opportunity of getting lifted and tossed around in the bedroom. It was why men who had weak and fragile arms were never her choice and they could never stand a chance with her. It was her equivalent for women who decided to look at shoes first; Heaven looked at arms.

Her lips finally parted as she spoke in a thin and rather unexpected tone. "Do you come here often?" The question sounded silly even to Heaven since she could swear she had seen Jazz in the gym many times. It was simply a conversation starter and a means to drag her away from being so flabbergasted by the girl's body. Jazz tilted her head from side to side as she replied. "Well, yeah, I come here about three times a week, and the other two days are used to work out at my team's gym."

Heaven found herself becoming even more intrigued by Jazz and whatever she was into. There was a hint of shyness in the manner she spoke, but her eloquence could not be disputed either.

"Team gym?" she asked curiously.

"Yes. I'm training with a team and aiming for a spot on the women's basketball team in Washington, DC," Jazz explained. "If I'm picked, I have to be fit."

Heaven's eyes widened, and she felt her heart thump slightly. She couldn't believe the thoughts running through her mind in that moment, but she wondered what it would be like to be married to someone in such a profession and enjoy the lavish lifestyle that came along with it.

Then she recalled the pay disparity between the NBA and WNBA and realized it might not be the fast ticket to easy meals she was assuming it would turn out to be for her. She just couldn't help herself; thinking a thousand steps ahead about ways to milk situations or even get the best out of deals.

She nudged herself out of her selfish and drowning thoughts, slowly warmed up to the exciting nature Jazz had brought over, and began to feel intrigued by her and everything that had to do with her.

Heaven suddenly pretended to struggle with the lat pull-down machine before her, encouraging Jazz to step closer to assist.

"I got that for you."

Her words were simply warming, and the manner in which she stepped forward was equally thrilling. It was within the twinkle of an eye. Heaven needed assistance, Jazz guided the machine up and down as Heaven's eyes continued to widen and marvel at her through the ensuing event. Jazz's entire body was fit as fiddle, and judging by the manner her joints moved effortlessly, Heaven felt some sting of desire and jealousy at the same time. No matter where Heaven was, whenever she set eyes on something she felt looked like a juicy piece of steak, she'd always try to picture what they'd look like if she let them tap that ass.

Heaven didn't sense any kind of muscular or bone issues so she found herself becoming more intrigued with Jazz.

"Oh, it's eight thirty!" Heaven exclaimed after realizing she had lost track of time. "I've got to get my baby girl, Hilly, and go!"

"You have a kid?" Jazz asked.

Heaven cocked her head in response. "Yes, a beautiful baby girl. She's my world."

"Wow! Where is she?"

"She's in the gym day care, but I don't introduce my

princess to strangers."

Jazz held up her hands to show she held no grudge and replied. "I respect that. So let me put my number in your phone, and you can call me when you're free. I want to finish helping you to customize your gym workout."

Heaven's eyes lit up with excitement. She felt rather naughty having met someone else who wanted to pay her some attention even though things weren't completely severed with Breezy. Heaven and Jazz exchanged numbers, and Heaven picked up Hilly and went home.

Heaven could barely believe her eyes as she walked into her house. It was late; she was dead tired. Having to return to the sight before her was just annoying.

"Get your white ass out of my bed! How the fuck could you be smoking weed!" Heaven felt her mood threaten to sour after having such a wonderful encounter with Jazz earlier.

"I'm not smoking weed. It's a rolled cigarette," Breezy replied.

"I don't give a fuck if it's rolled monkey ass, just get it out of my bedroom!" she replied before storming off.

"I was trying to set a mood for you! All you see is me in bed smoking. Did you even see the roses? Did you see the Chinese food? Did you even notice the house was clean?" Breezy was annoyed because he was trying his best to create an intimate evening for the two of them. "I told you to stop referring to me like a racist, Heaven. I don't want my daughter growing up being a racist—like her racist-ass mother! If I came home and called you a black-ass bitch, I would be wrong. Stop referring to me as white anything. I know I'm white, just like I know you're black. But apparently on some level my race is a problem for you.

It didn't stop you from wanting my seed, though… Give me my daughter."

Heaven, feeling convicted about being so nasty to Breezy, handed Hilly over to Breezy. Breezy and Hilly went into the living room and left Heaven in the room alone for the rest of the night.

The next morning, the routine began. Since Breezy was there, he woke up early to take Hilly to day care and Heaven to work.

Heaven always arrived at work on time when she got a ride. Breezy had a lot of fucked-up qualities, but some of his white qualities were dominant. He hated tardiness. He hated that sometimes Heaven valued her time over his and others, so whenever he had an opportunity to control their arrivals anywhere he made sure that they were on time.

It was a little windy and rainy on this particular morning, and Heaven walked briskly in the office building. As she entered the building, she picked up the pace to make sure she was at her desk before supervisor "dick" started making his rounds, when she suddenly slipped on her ass.

Yes, the floor of the office building was wet, and she had just experienced a slip-and-fall accident.

Heaven stayed on the ground until she saw someone coming. In a matter of minutes, Heaven already knew she had a lawsuit.

A fucking slip-and-fall, and it was caught on camera. As soon as Heaven made eye contact with someone else entering the lobby, she started crying and saying, "Help me. I can't get up." By this time, several people had arrived and the ambulance had been called. Word had spread around the building that there was a slip and fall. The ambulance and maintenance crew arrived at the same time.

Building management had also arrived on the scene, trying to offer Heaven assistance. Heaven knew that if she wanted a case, she'd need to go to the hospital. She refused help from building management and took a trip to the hospital by ambulance. On the way to the hospital, Heaven called her mom and Breezy; both rushed to the hospital to be by her side. Heaven, who'd never really had a back injury, didn't know how to pretend that she had one. When she fell, she didn't hurt herself to the point of requiring an ambulance. If anything, she hurt her ego by falling on her ass in a cute dress and pumps!

Heaven was released from the hospital several hours later with strong painkillers and a referral to see her primary care doctor in a few days. She had no intention to see her primary care doctor. On the next business day, she was going to see a lawyer. Since Heaven experienced an injury en route to work, supervisor "dick," Alexander, granted her one-week off from work.

She had no intention of returning in one week, and during her time off she had started applying for better positions closer to home.

Within a week, Heaven had won again! She landed an interview at a organization in Washington, DC. who had secured major govern contracts.

Not only that, she found a reputable personal injury lawyer who had a reputation for making something out of nothing. Heaven went to her job interview at 10 a.m. and went to see the lawyer at 2 p.m. the same day. Heaven was always two steps ahead. Whenever she set her mind to do something, all of her energy was directed toward that goal, and she generally crushed all of her goals. This new government contractor position was a step in the right direction. However, with this new job came a significant salary increase, and a salary increase meant she had to report her new salary to the DC Housing Authority.

As much as Heaven loved the benefits of Section 8, she hated the embarrassment of having her employers complete paperwork verifying her salary. She didn't want HR in her business. This was a huge motivator for Heaven to do whatever it took to get off of Section 8, but for now she still needed it.

Weeks had gone by without her communicating with

Jazz. Breezy was around a bit more because she had to keep up the charade with her back injury, and Heaven's mom was sitting back watching her daughter work, making everything always go in her favor. Heaven had a knack for always winning people over in an effort to advance her cause.

If only Heaven could settle down, get off Section 8, achieve financial freedom, and get rid of Breezy once and for all—she'd be living her life like it's golden.

Heaven glared at Breezy, unsure of how best to confront her emotions as she took another sniff and decided she was right; the air lingered with perfume, and not the masculine kind, either. There was no proof another woman had come into the room or into her house because she had not met any, but the feeling had grown over the past week alone, and she could not discard it any longer.

Becoming restless, unsure of what to do and uncertain of how best to confront the man who continued to mess his life up, she got up from the bed, walked over to the stacks of boxes Breezy had brought along during her move, and began to pore through them. Heaven wasn't quite of what she was searching for, but her heart needed answers, and she wondered if she would at least find one.

She rummaged through the old boxes, almost tore them apart as she thought of the times she had returned home and smelled the stench of feminine perfume in her house. She had not confronted Breezy because she was worried he would get mad and she didn't want to be wrong. More so, he still assisted in keeping the routine of dropping Hilly off and transporting her to and from work.

Her mind raged with the notion that he was cheating, but she didn't want to believe it for any reason until she finally came across a box filled with old gadgets, which Breezy often seemed protective about.

With thoughts of destroying them in a bid to pay him back for the mental torture he was trapping her in, she plunged her hand into the box and felt what appeared to be a cell phone. Curious, she took it out, had a good look at it, and turned it on, only to realize it still worked as she clamped her thumb down and hard onto the power button. Slowly, the phone booted up and the screen came to life. It lingered on for a minute as she flicked through it, but suddenly went flat due to poor battery life. Heaven searched through the box some more and finally located the charger. Anxious, she raced over to the power outlet closest to her and plugged it in. The phone came back on, and Heaven began to scroll through the files on it.

It didn't take long to spot prerecorded videos in it that left her aghast.

Her hands trembled, and her eyes slowly watered as she watched the painful sight of Breezy having sex with not just one, but with three women. She scrolled through, checked the dates attached to them, and felt her heart continue to sink. It was surreal to witness, and there was no amount of reasoning she could apply to the videos that could grant her calm. *Oh my God!* she thought. One of the dates was particularly troubling because it was precisely a day after her daughter, Hilly, was born.

"That motherfucker!" She was filled with rage as she got to her feet and kicked the stool before her. She crumpled to the ground with a loud heave and began to weep profusely at the fact she had been blind and ignorant of Breezy's true nature.

He had been playing her, and she wondered what more or how much more he had done without her noticing. She cringed and swore underneath her breath, but nothing seemed to calm her down. She wanted out, or as far away from everything as possible.

In lieu of this, Heaven reached for her cell phone, scrolled through her chat log, and came across a weekend getaway some colleagues at work had been planning.

"I'm in," she replied. She needed a way to clear her mind, and going on the trip to Miami seemed like the perfect response.

Chapter 12
MIA in Miami

Heaven stood before the mirror for the last time and admired how beautiful she looked. Her hair hung atop her shoulders, and her eyes shimmered in the mirror as she smiled and sighed at the same time.

The images she had seen and videos she watched on Breezy's old phone continued to haunt her; she had barely been able to have proper sleep during her trip down to Miami. She felt alone, in need of someone to speak with, and definitely burdened at heart as well.

"Babe! Come on! Stop sulking, or you're going to miss the show!" one of the girls screamed from the other side of the door.

Heaven slowly dragged herself back into consciousness upon realizing she had lost track of time completely. For the past hour, she had been in the bathroom crying and soiling her gorgeous face because she worried Breezy's actions would impact her daughter.

"I'm coming," she said, and wiped her face clean and stepped out of the bathroom. Heaven looked absolutely stunning. Her short red dress was mesmerizing to anyone's sight, and her slender, fresh-looking legs screamed for attention as she walked down the hallway. "You really know how to bring it, girl!" one of the four girls she had come to Miami with screamed.

"We definitely need to have some fun tonight!" another yelled, pumping her fist into the air. Heaven wanted something other than fun. Fun would limit her mind from thinking about the issues plaguing her, but she wanted something more.

No sooner had she walked into the club with the other four girls did her cell phone ring. Reluctant to pick it up, more calls continued to come through until she felt compelled to pick up and answer the call.

"Hello, Heaven." The unmistakable voice came through, and Heaven felt all her worries melt away. She jumped to her feet, felt her breath suddenly become heavy and laden, and her mood improved, without a doubt.

"Hey, Jazz!" she said, and raced out of the club to a more secluded and quiet place. Heaven could not believe her ears, but hearing from Jazz felt like the tonic she needed in that moment.

"How are you and how is Miami? Someone decided to ride off without involving me, and it's leaving me a little bit jealous over here," Jazz said.

Heaven let off a thin smile, held back her breath, and

without realizing it, broke down in tears.

"Hey, what is going on?" Jazz asked, sounding compassionate as she lent a listening ear to Heaven.

Heaven sniffed, held back her words, and decided against pouring out her soul or dumping her worries on Jazz.

Instead, she would rather indulge Jazz in some lighthearted talk and hopefully find some way to feel happy.

"Well, if you aren't going to tell me what's been bothering you, I initially called to tell you I actually missed you and would love to have you around as much as possible," Jazz said boldly.

The words brought Heaven a smile and tendered her heart too. She would love to be around Jazz in that moment as well. Something about her just brought a soothing relief and seemed to cast aside her worries for a moment.

Heaven would spend the remainder of her trip speaking with Jazz and barely even granting herself time to have fun as she had intended. Jazz seemed like everything she wanted in that moment, and she undoubtedly felt like the world she had been searching for too.

Heaven returned from Miami a day sooner than the others had planned.

She wasn't having as much fun as she wanted, and the thoughts of having her daughter far away while she jollied wasn't sitting nicely with her, either. It was easier when she felt she could trust Breezy with their child, but not anymore. In fact, she was slowly becoming certain of not wanting anything to do with him, but there was the issue on how it was bound to affect her daughter.

With an exhaustive sigh, she reached for the doorknob into her apartment and found the door was unlocked. Breezy had a spare key; she figured he was in, and her emotions began to go through another cesspool of madness. She took a moment to breathe and take her time to recount her thoughts and gain some proper composure before finally opening the door and walking into the room.

The air was thick with an unsavory scent, and the living room was a junky hot mess. The furniture was moved out of place, clothes hung everywhere from the couch to the television, and strange sounds emanated from her bedroom.

Heaven's heart slumped as she could very well guess what it was she was hearing.

Oh my God! she thought, cringing inside and unsure of how best to proceed.

Her legs seemed to stiffen, and her knees wouldn't move. She looked around, waited to summon enough courage before marching to her bedroom and shoving the door open. The sight left her in tatters as she glared at Breezy having sex with two women. The world seemed to stop in that instance, and she held her breath, unsure of how best to proceed. Luckily Hilly was sound asleep in the next room and unbothered by the shenanigans in the next room.

"Breezy," she mumbled, unsure of what act to take next, but she could feel herself swelling on the inside.

Breezy looked lost and barely saw what was coming as Heaven lunged at one of the ladies whom she had seen in one of the previous videos on Breezy's phone.

She pulled at the lady's hair and managed to drag her out of the bedroom.

"You fucking tricks , get your rags for clothes and get the fuck out of my house!"

Breezy hurriedly got himself clothed and raced to Heaven in the living room.

"How the fuck could you bring those tramps into my house, you fucking good-for-nothing white-ass bastard!" Heaven yelled. "How could you?"

Breezy fell silent, parted his lips to defend himself, but had no words to say.

"I saw those videos you made with those hoes, by the way," she informed him. "I saw them on your phone, and you should be ashamed of yourself, sleeping with random women a day after your daughter was born! Yeah I know all about that jackass."

"You went through my phone?" he asked. "You fucking snooped through my things?"

Heaven scoffed, noting how he was on the verge of turning the entire thing around. She wasn't having any of his nonsense, though. She had seen enough to know better, and she wasn't about to let herself become used.

"Get out of my house. I don't want to see you right

now, or I will call the cops on your corny white ass!" She knew the racial statement would irk him, and gladly so. Breezy, defeated, slowly retreated and exited the house without a fuss.

Heaven locked the door behind him and slumped to the ground and burst into tears. She felt burned and drained of strength to cry.

"Why?" she asked. She needed an answer to why things always seemed to run downhill for her.

She had Jazzy on one hand, who was doing her best to ensure life was filled with happiness and good mood for Heaven.

Breezy's issues just continued to irk and render Heaven emotionally unstable.

Two weeks had gone past since Heaven first found Breezy in her bed with other women, and things had not taken a better turn.

Her mother had decided against getting involved, citing the need for Heaven to find her own truth, while Jazz remained supportive and absolutely wonderful.

They still had not seen or even had time to be together since all the madness ensued.

Heaven stepped out of her workplace after working late to the sight of Breezy standing by his truck. He had not come to pick her up since they last argued, which was a week before, and his presence wasn't welcome.

"What do you want?" Heaven asked.

"I want to know where the fuck my daughter is," he said.

She scoffed and stepped to the side so she could leave, but he remained adamant and continued to pester her. An argument broke off once again, just as it had every time they spoke on phone and the last time they saw.

"You really think getting all up in my face after acting like a goddamn prostitute is key?" she asked. "You shame not just yourself but your daughter as well."

Breezy fumed and his faced seemed to become redder as Heaven heard her phone ring. She reached inside her purse to pick up her call. Breezy snatched her cell phone, rammed it to the ground, and clenched his fists as she squared up to him without an ounce of fear in her eyes.

"That's the height to what I will take from you! You have no respect for me, for my things, or even my life!" she raged. "Go to hell! It's over."

Breeze sniffed, almost as if he sensed things were coming to that already, and shook his head.

"Fuck you!" he yelled while he retreated to his truck.

Distraught and definitely not what she had envisaged, or even wanted for her daughter, Heaven could not believe the remarkably emotional weeks she had been having.

Growing up without a father, she knew the impact it

had on her, and she didn't want that for her daughter. The breakup would definitely stand, but she was open to allowing Breezy to have a part to play in her daughter's life again.

She went on her knees, picked up her battered cell phone with teary eyes as she heard a car pull up in front of her. Heaven looked up to see Jazz behind the wheel with a heartwarming smile.

"I had a feeling you needed me, and even while this seems creepy, showing up at your workplace without notice, I think being here is right," Jazz said.

Heaven could not deny how elated she was to see Jazz. "I was calling to tell you I'd like to come pick you up, but your phone went dead."

Heaven showed her the broken phone, and without saying a single word got into the car before they drove away.

Later that evening

Jittery, to say the least, Heaven danced across the room, hoping and praying she was on track. A lot was definitely riding on the night turning out well, and there was no denying just how worried she was.

Heaven hurried through the living room, sweating profusely as she struggled to calm down or get herself into her usual composed self.

A romantic date with Jazz meant everything to her, and everything had to be perfect.

The breakup with Breezy aside, she had not been that tense in a very long time.

She decided that she simply didn't want him in her life; they agreed to co-parent their daughter.

Date Night with Jazz

"What am I missing? What am I missing?" Heaven asked herself as she grew extremely nervous. Her nervousness had begun from that car ride with Jazz on the afternoon she needed a savior and she had shown up.

In fact, hearing Jazz ask for a proper date had almost had Heaven choking before she nodded her head and hurriedly agreed. She had never been on a date with a woman in such context before, and Jazz definitely didn't seem like she was shying away from what she wanted. She set the dining table and ensured the entire room smelled nice (like coconut to be exact) before rushing to the shower to clean up and get dressed.

Heaven opted for her purple strapless "freakum" dress, which stood just some inches above her knee. Her makeup was light and sensual, and her heartbeat was heavy as images of Jazz poured through her mind.

She was about to indulge herself with a woman she was now certain wasn't like any other she had met. In fact, Jazz's warmth and kindness had become a factor in becoming close and liking of her.

Heaven glanced at the wall clock and realized she

was just about ten minutes from her date with Jazz.

"Shit! Candles! Candles! Where are the freaking candles?" Heaven said as she was about to have a meltdown. She raced through the room, searching for the candles before hearing the doorbell ring. Her heart leaped as she finally found them and lit them appropriately across the dinner table. "Keep your calm, Heaven. Keep your calm," she muttered to herself as she hurried to the front door. She counted her breath once again, hovered her hand atop the doorknob, before finally turning the doorknob and standing before the most beautiful girl she had seen in her life.

"Hello, gorgeous," the lady in red pants, perfectly glossed lips, and mild makeup said as she gazed into Heaven's eyes.

Heaven felt every single worry she ever harbored until then melt away without a trace.

"Hello…" Heaven struggled for words before the unexpected happened.

Jazz leaned over, slipped her cherry-tasting lips between Heaven's, causing the latter's eyes to widen and her breath to cease almost immediately.

The lips remained locked for a moment, and Heaven felt like heaven had fallen upon her before Jazz slowly pulled away. Slowly, she stepped aside, led Jazz into the room in hopes they would not have just a wonderful date night but a perfect one too. The night would turn out to be absolutely much more than Heaven had planned or even wished for. She'd not only get love and affection, but confirmation the next morning for a ***new job offer*** to work with the federal government, with a pay raise of $15,000, which she accepted.

Bye-Bye Section 8.

Chapter 13
I Hate Working for Women

It had been two days into the job, after the endless vetting process and trainings that Heaven thought would never come to an end. She was where she wanted to be, a corner office overlooking the city, with the most exquisite furnishings she had even been around. It was expected, seeing she was taking the role of *Special Assistant to the Director of Human Resources* in federal government agency. Heaven finally achieved her goals of becoming a federal employee.

The appointment was amazing, to say the least, and the swearing-in was wonderful as well.

Her work colleagues weren't the typical set, and they definitely seemed to know where they stood as they welcomed her and promptly resumed at their workstations.

Jazz's call came through while Heaven allowed herself to drown in the beauty of the moment. "Babe, so how is it going?" Jazz asked immediately, purring from where she was. Heaven couldn't quite believe her eyes or anything going on around her, but since her decision to leave Breezy, it felt as though she had been threading on one good thing to another.

"I got a corner office," Heaven replied. "I got the best office on the floor! Can you imagine?"

Jazz clapped her hands wildly from the other side before replying. "You deserve the best, babe, and I think it calls for another celebration tonight." Heaven smiled to herself and shook her head. The events from the previous dinner still played through her mind. The date was perfect, Jazz was impeccable in character, and the night was the best she had had in a while. In fact, she had looked forward to having another night to share with Jazz ever since. "Well, we could make something happen tonight." Heaven sounded eager. "Someone seems super anxious." Jazz chuckled. "Well, I have a surprise for you tonight." Heaven felt the desire to push, but she didn't want to ruin the surprise.

Jazz would come through for sure, and she was beginning to sense that.

"I got to go for now," Heaven whispered into her phone as she saw a lady walking toward her office through the glass wall. Heaven was certain she had not met the lady before, but something about the manner in which she was marching over sent shivers down her spine.

"If it isn't the new girl on the block," the woman said as soon as she walked into the office. She took a look around, almost as if she was searching for something, before leaning into Heaven's desk and looking at her in a rather odd manner.

"Good morning. How may I help you?" Heaven asked politely.

The lady scoffed derisively and shook her head. "How can someone like you help me?" Those words didn't come with the same cordial intent Heaven had hoped she would get in return, but she remained silent. "Well, you can help me by ensuring my office is well kept, my coffee is served, and that you don't miss my meetings, think you are better than I am, or even attempt to in any way demean my authority," she stated.

Heaven swallowed hard, wondering if she was standing before another version of Pedro Perez. She ground her teeth and refused to utter a response as she stood there in silence. "I hear your name is Heaven (*I hope your ass isn't here to make my life hell* Heaven thought), and while you got introduced to the team yesterday, I was at a meeting, so I will introduce myself to you," the woman said.

"My name is Kanisha Wislou, and I am one of the most dangerous persons to mess with around here." Heaven didn't find herself feeling scared for any reason at all. Instead, she bobbed her head in the moment, hoping to agree with the woman and hopefully see her leave. "Are you married?" she asked Heaven.

Heaven shook her head.

"I thought as much," the rude lady remarked before turning around. "I expect you to come running when I call you, by the way, newbie." Heaven gave the entire ordeal some thought and decided it was best she sorted things right away rather than enslave herself to another version of Pedro Perez. "I'm sorry, but I work for the Director of Human Resources, and it clearly states it on my application letter that—" Heaven tried to explain her case and separate herself from other positions in the office.

Wislou turned around with a frown and held her lips open as if she wanted to speak for a moment. Heaven stopped talking too.

"Looks like we got ourselves a sassy mouth black Barbie," Wislou said with a frown.

Heaven took no offense in the racial word because Wislou was black too, but the tone with which she spoke was definitely bothersome.

"Mrs. Wislou!" someone called from the hallway, prompting the annoying looking woman to turn away and head right out. Heaven took a look at who had called her and caused her to abandon the trouble she was about to create. It turned out to be the Director of HR. The man simply waved toward Heaven, paused for a moment, and began to walk her way.

Shit! Heaven thought as she straightened her dress and watched the man walk in.

Mr. Greenstein, a cheery fellow often fond of donning a smile, shook hands with Heaven before looking out of her office window for a moment as if he was trying to look for something.

"I see you've gotten acquainted with your office and

Mrs. Wislou," he said with a grin.

Heaven nodded her head. "Lovely woman." Mr. Greenstein smiled and shook his head. "I wouldn't be that charitable, but you should have fun working here. Watch your back, darling." It undoubtedly sounded like she was being warned, but she took the advice and decided to set about work promptly. The day was still fresh, and she wanted to give a lasting impression. It was her first few days at work, after all.

Heaven walked into the general cafeteria to the sight of other workers like herself, suddenly going numb and the entire atmosphere going flat as though she had sucked it all away. She felt nervous for a moment but soon decided to keep walking before the whisperings and endless murmurings began to ensure. She could hear her name being mentioned, but for reasons she couldn't quite tell yet.

What on earth is going on? Heaven thought as she settled down to have her meal. The minutes she was there felt like hours, and the longer she remained there, the more difficult it felt to ignore the fact she was the talk of the entire floor.

She looked herself through to ensure she wasn't sporting a shabby look, but she was good and nothing was out of place.

"Freaking bitch!" Heaven heard someone mumble.

Her mood definitely slumped as she got to her feet and abandoned her meal. She headed down the hallway and hoped to return to her office, where she didn't have to be with anyone for a while.

"We don't trick our managers here, and we sure as hell don't sneak our way into getting our jobs," a foul-mouthed lady said as Heaven walked past. It didn't take long for everything to connect. Heaven realized they were referring to how she had gotten her previous job at the law firm and the issues she was accused of as well. *What the hell do they know? Who on earth is spreading such damaging information?*

Heaven wondered, looking perplexed as she returned to her office. Standing at the end of the corridor, staring her way with a wry smile and an evil grin was none other than Wislou. *That ugly bitch did this*, Heaven realized. It was obvious she alone had the power to seek out such information, and she obviously had a grudge against Heaven.

Heaven had not taken it into account, Wislou's awful look only made her look even more irritating. Her short, unappealing self repulsed Heaven, but Heaven wasn't about to allow her drain what happy mood she had been compiling through the day.

"Take in deep breaths. You will be fine," Heaven assured herself as she turned away and headed to her office. She sat on her chair, flicked on her computer, and watched the screen blur for a moment before puff of smoke eased out from its sides. "No…no…no…no!" Heaven yelled, realizing the work she had spent half the morning doing was gone.

Considering the computer was new and in perfect working condition, Heaven could not make sense of what had happened. She lowered her head in anger and frustration, feeling a headache slowly begin to slip in, before deciding she would find another way to make things work. She walked out of her office to seek assistance from other colleagues. They all seemed reluctant, except one lady.

Mrs. Ellen Harrison smiled at Heaven and groped her hand tightly as she led her away from the crowd and into the photocopy room. "Wislou has her eyes on you," the elderly woman said.

"I don't understand," Heaven replied.

"You don't need to, but everyone in this office know her to be nuts.

"Everyone avoids her and hates her, but nobody has been able to get her terminated." the woman said.

"She is smart, though, and well revered, but tread carefully."

Heaven had no choice but to believe the woman had definitely sabotaged her computer.

"I haven't done anything to her, Heaven claimed in innocence.

Mrs. Ellen chuckled and replied. "Keep your office locked at all times, watch your back, and don't get in her crosshairs." It was the most vital piece of information Heaven would be granted on that day, and one she had to abide by through her stay there.

Later that evening

"Can you please leave work and just be in the moment with me?" Jazz pleaded in her naturally gleeful manner as she smiled at Heaven. Heaven reached across the table and held Jazz's hand with the most soothing relief. Her tender hand, her calming presence, and loving aura granted Heaven everything she needed in that moment.

"Since Hilly is now asleep, I believe it's time to fulfill my surprise," Jazz said before getting up from her seat.

She walked over to her messenger bag and returned with a jewelry box, which she presented to Heaven while she crouched near Heaven's legs. Heaven looked into Jazz's eyes and then back at the box. "No, you shouldn't have."

"Go on and open it. You deserve the finest things," Jazz said.

Heaven unwrapped the gift box and felt her world almost flip upside down when she saw the signature Tiffany box and opened it.

"Tiffany bracelets and earrings?" she asked, taking another good look at them as though they weren't real.

She leaped up from her seat, pulled Jazz closer, and wrapped her arms around her. Tenderly, Heaven locked lips with the woman she was really beginning to feel so much for and very comfortable with, while they both ignored the perfectly set dinner on the dining table.

"I guess I have something for you as well." Heaven smiled.

Jazz raised her right brow, wondering what it was as Heaven led her out of the living room and into the bedroom. Underneath the watchful eye of the blue-rimmed moon outside the window, Jazz and Heaven shared a really hot and passionate night together for the first time.

Amazed by the wonderful passion-filled love making session they had shared a few nights before, Heaven continued to bite her lower lip as she replayed the moments she had Jazz's nipples between her lips.

Her entire body had been nothing short of magical, and the taste she could still recall from running her tongue through every inch of it was wonderful.

Heaven, in that moment, believed nothing could go wrong for the remainder of the week. In fact, she had woken up late, with Jazz by her side and the warm scent of their bodies entwining the night before.

The following morning

Loud cluttering noises and verbal exchanges of displeasure and happiness all mixed into one brought

Heaven back into the present as she took note of people standing before the office bulletin board looking at who had been approved for the coveted training program.

People seemed to glare at her for a moment but soon eased off as Heaven innocently and ignorantly walked to her office.

She had just gotten to the door when she felt her bag and folder drop from her hand. It was definitely surreal to look at, and it caused her heart to skip its beats.

"Oh my God!" she exclaimed.

Her office was a mess, and it looked as though someone had intentionally damaged her computer, her chair, and even the walls. It was an impossible sight to even look at, and the longer she stood there to glare at the reality before her, the more troubling it felt to her soul. Her mind raced to one person and one alone, but there was no proof and no way to really pin it on her. And more importantly Heaven was denied an opportunity to attend a very critical training program.

Wislou walked past soon enough, acted as though she had not seen Heaven's trashed office before calling on her. Her vile nature wasn't in any way comparable with how ugly she was, and it made Heaven want to punch her in the face. She needed to keep her cool and not land herself in hot soup as she did with Pedro Perez.

"What's funny?" Heaven asked.

"Well, I assess and deem people and their level of qualifications in this office, and you just don't cut it and will not cut it for any reason as long as I work here," she replied.

Heaven knew just what to do, and without uttering any more words or even implicating herself, she rushed past Wislou and headed for the director of HR's office immediately. "Good morning, Miss Davis." Mr. Greenstein greeted her with a smile as soon as Heaven entered his office. She went right to the point, without holding back. Within minutes, Wislou was called into his office.

"May I ask why Miss Heaven's name was not on the list of trainees yet you approved many others?" he asked. Wislou's eyes narrowed and it was easy to see the hate in there as she replied. "We had some issues with funding, and I made the decision to cut her out for now."

It wasn't hard to note it was a lie, but Heaven watched as Mr. Greenstein mandated that Heaven be reinstated promptly. The duo walked out of that office with one party being happy and the other mad as hell. Heaven didn't care at all; she got the good end of the deal.

Spending the day sorting her office again and ensuring her work items were restored was a rather tasking ordeal, but meeting Jazz at the gym where they had planned to hang out was something she looked forward to.

Heaven had just gotten off the bus with Hilly when she received an email tagged from Wislou.

"You black piece of shit, going off to meet with the director

and thinking you can get one over me is just laughable. I will personally make life a living hell for you, ensure you drown before you even attempt to paddle and when I am done with you, there will be nothing left. Watch your back you whore!"

The email broke her heart, and more came through almost immediately with more vile words and more hostility being displayed in every single one of them.

"Hey!" Jazz waved Heaven over as she walked across the room to meet with the sexy lady. "Work trouble again?" Heaven nodded her head before putting away the phone so she could enjoy some proper time with Jazz. "What do you do when you constantly get bullied by a colleague who everyone is so scared of that nobody has been able to get her sacked from office?" Heaven asked. She had done a little research on Wislou, and it turned out that the woman often threatened anyone who attempted to get her kicked out of office with an EEO complaint.

It seemed to have worked for years and was the reason she remained in office as well. "Then you don't allow them to bully you, honey," Jazz replied before pulling Heaven closer and planting a kiss on her forehead. "You aren't a wussy, and you shouldn't let some ugly bitch put you down."

It was really troubling to have someone as ugly as Wislou giving her such a tough time. "Come on, let's work out and have some fun." Jazz pulled her along as they headed off to drop off Hilly so the couple would have time to themselves. The gym session was beyond amazing, and Heaven liked the fact Jazz had a way of pushing her toward getting better.

Considering how busy Jazz was, it was even more calming for Heaven to have her around because she provided a shoulder to cry on as well as listening ears for Heaven and her problems. It was even more remarkable since Jazz was an entrepreneur who owned three all-natural smoothie drink bars in Washington, DC.

Heaven just could not thank her stars enough for coming across Jazz, and when it was time for them to part ways after working out, it felt like an impossible thing to do.

"See you in a couple of days," Jazz whispered into Heaven's ear before planting a bold kiss on her lips in the parking lot. Heaven waved good-bye and turned around to go wait at the spot for Breezy, who would often come pick up Hilly when it was his turn to be with her. Oddly enough, Heaven noticed no one other than Wislou, looking quite drunk in in the TGI Friday's parking lot next to the gym wearing a short leather skirt getting into the car with a male colleague – after planting a seductive kiss on his lips. In utter disbelief, Heaven snapped a few pictures knowing she had stumbled onto something good.

Meanwhile

Breezy and Heaven agreed he'd have her for the next

two days, and Heaven had decided to be busy during that period.

"This is what you do with my child?" Breezy asked as he stepped out of the shadows.

Heaven was caught off guard, and the longer she stared at Breezy, the more apparent it was that she had no response to give him. Yet she wasn't threatened, but more or less worried about Jazz being dragged into anything she was working through with Breezy.

"What I do with my life isn't your business," Heaven warned.

"It is my business if my daughter is being made to see it!" Breezy replied.

Heaven sighed, feeling tired of being on the defensive as she looked at Hilly.

She wanted the best for her daughter, and she definitely wanted her daughter to act in a way that showed her mother had always taught her to have spine.

"You can go to hell," Heaven whispered, turned away, and decided she wasn't allowing him to have their child for the night. It would be a lesson to him, and she didn't care what the consequences would be.

"I will sue for child custody and leave your horny ass chasing that bitch I just saw you kissing!" Breezy threatened.

She had no doubt he would sue, but she would give up her life before she was going to allow anyone have her daughter.

Two Weeks Later

Heaven wasn't on the verge of letting Wislou have the better say this time around. Having to walk into the office and seeing someone else being drafted into her workplace was like an insult to her very face.

"Your career is done! It is finished, right here and now!" Wislou assured Heaven as she marched off.

"Well, the joke is on you, bitch, because I will be ruining yours first!" Heaven retorted.

People had gathered, and the sight was overwhelming. People couldn't believe their eyes seeing Heaven stand up to someone in the frame and mold of Kanisha Wislou.

Mr. Greenstein appeared and stood stiff as he watched the ladies continue to go at each other.

"You two! In my office this instant!" he demanded. Heaven walked into the office, beaming with a smile on her face and with a great deal of confidence. She took her seat, as did her counterpart before Mr. Greenstein did the same.

"Can you tell me why you two turned the entire office into something of a spectacle?" he asked, looking enraged.

Wislou went first, citing the need to air her views as the superior.

"This thot right here constantly demeans my authority. She constantly abuses me as her superior, and I cannot work with her and no longer want her working anywhere near this office." Heaven took a moment to breathe before closing her eyes and thinking through everything she had been doing for the past two weeks.

Quite frankly, Heaven had planned for a moment such as the one she was having now. She had counted the days and carefully put her pieces into place before confronting Wislou that very morning. It was the only way to prevent the callous, hostile lady from sabotaging not just her work any further, but from sabotaging her future as well. "Is this true, Miss Davis?" Mr. Greenstein asked.

Heaven cleared her throat and replied as boldly as she could. "No, sir. But I'd like to report that Mrs. Wislou has continually made this work environment not just hostile towards me, but a volatile one as well, and I have ample proof which I have collected over the past two weeks to attest to this." Wislou's face seemed to drop in that moment, but Heaven didn't care and continued to look away.

"Lies! Absolutely lies!" Wislou yelled.

Mr. Greenstein rubbed his temple before asking Heaven to provide evidence she had to corroborate her accusations.

"If you can back this up, I will deal with you both for such a level of unprofessionalism shown out there today," Mr. Greenstein warned. Heaven cocked her head, placed her cell phone on the table with her emails open to be viewed, before picking up the official complaint form sitting on the desk in front of her. Looking at the terrified vile woman to her right, Heaven said, "I have photos that may be of interest to you sir."

I believe government's policy in work environment doesn't permit any form of sexual indulgence with colleagues."

Wislou looked aghast, and her face whitened. Heaven smirked and showed a thin smile in the corner of her mouth before getting up. She was certain there was no way Wislou was getting out of trouble this time around. It definitely wasn't going to happen, with all the proof she had gathered over the last two weeks.

An hour passed, and after a sharp lecturing from Greenstein, Wislou walked out of her office with what she could take of her belongings in a box she carried.

She was put on administrative leave indefinitely. She looked dejected and barely looked up as people lined the hallway to see her eventually walk out of the building. Heaven sat in her office, legs crossed, eyes fixated on Wislou as she left the floor. She felt a sense of pride and vindication filling her chest. She had just prevailed against a major office bully, and she knew it.

Even without Mr. Greenstein's phone call, which came in minutes later to apologize on behalf of the office for such hostile working conditions she was being subjected to and the harassment Mrs. Wislou dealt her, Heaven was swimming in her victory. "We are sincerely sorry, and on behalf of everyone, I promise this and nothing like it will ever happen again," he said.

The truth was, Heaven had accepted her fate and ordeal. She had other things plaguing her mind right now. What business she could do and how well she can make it as an entrepreneur? Working people like Wislou and Perez had sucked the wind out her, and she wasn't sure she wanted to keep working for anyone ever again other than for herself.

Even if she had to work for someone else, she was determined it wouldn't be an ugly-ass bitch, or a woman, for that matter.

Chapter 14
Love & Stability

Fuming red in the face, barely able to maintain a coordinated breath, Breezy paced without actually knowing where to stand or what to do. Breezy, who had been watching things unfold before his very eyes for the past few weeks and had had just about enough and felt it was time to let things out.

His clenched fists balled with anger, and his eyes remained fixated on the door ahead, while he tried to hold his breath and keep his calm. The fact was, it just wasn't working. It wasn't going to be, and the longer he had to stay there, waiting for "her," the more enraged he became.

"They must see me as an idiot of some kind," he mumbled to himself.

"They must see me as a fool of some kind."

The thoughts alone were maddening, and he needed a solution really soon.

Yet it felt as though Jazz was taking forever to come out. He saw her walk into the store an hour ago, and it left

Breezy with the thought of actually walking right in to confront her.

The one problem was how huge the store was. He might walk in through one door and miss her when she was walking out through another door. It was why he had decided to choose the most comfortable spot for himself, by her car, a black top of the line Range Rover. Tailing her had not been a hard task in any way. Considering all he had to do was to follow her from Heaven's house, where she had spent the night, it was easy as pie.

"Come out, bitch!" he mumbled to himself, folding his right hand into a fist and hammering it into the other palm. "Come out right now!"

The wait was becoming too long, the hot sun wasn't helping, and standing in a parking lot without actually doing anything could attract unwanted attention.

It just wasn't the time for him. It wasn't the time at all. "Finally!" He gasped, almost punching the air in what he could only describe to be triumph. Jazz, whom he had spent an hour and more waiting for, had finally emerged from the store.

She walked gracefully, seemingly unaware of what she had done to irk Breezy, or even that he had tailed her to the store. He glanced at her properly this time around and watched the object of his troubles standing not too far from him. Ever since the night he saw her kiss Heaven in the gym parking lot, his world had felt like it fell into shambles. Irreparable harm had been done to his ego. Breezy walked over to the tall-framed lady, stood by her, and looked her right in the face. "You must be Jazz."

Jazz gawked at him with some measure of loss in her eyes. She stepped to the side, hoping to avoid the confrontation, but Breezy wasn't having any of it. "Bitch, I'm speaking to you!" he said in a rude and rather uncouth manner. Jazz fastened her hand around her shopping bags and looked right back at Breezy, without knowing what to do.

Her truck was just a few feet away, but getting to it now felt and seemed impossible. "I don't know who you are, and I don't know what your deal is, but I'd kindly ask you to watch your mouth and step aside so I can access my truck," she said respectfully. Breezy smirked, scoffed, and spat to the side unruly. "I am Heaven's man. The chick you've been doing behind my back, you freaking lesbo!"

Breezy couldn't help himself. Everything he had seen the other night played in his mind and wouldn't stop. The nights that followed were tormenting.

The ability to indulge in anything other than thinking about what Heaven might be doing with Jazz was impossible. It was safe to say he was in abject misery, and the longer it went, the more desperate he was about doing something about the situation. Jazz's face definitely reddened, and while she wasn't speaking yet, it wasn't hard to tell she was beginning to feel appalled by the situation and by Breezy's words and the manner in which he spoke to her.

"I will give you one chance to apologize for talking shit and to get the hell out of my way champ," she warned.

Breezy spat to the ground again, almost meeting her leg this time around. It was definitely the height of the conflict, and she had had just about enough. Barely seeing it coming until it rammed hard on the left side of his face, Breezy took some steps backwards from the effect of Jazz's slap. He held his hurt face, which had reddened badly and had an imprint of her hand, while he stared at her in disbelief.

He had just been bitch-slapped by Jazz.

"Fuck off and go to hell, you weak bastard!" she said, heightening her voice in the process before sidestepping and finally gaining access to her truck.

"Come at me again, and I will drag your irresponsible and absolutely stupid ass to jail."

Breezy stood there, perplexed and as if an avalanche had struck him.

Jazz had slapped the shit out of him with those strong WNBA arms and hands, and he only then began to give everything proper thought after her truck zoomed off into the distance. Breezy headed for the police station, the to DC Superior Court. Jazz definitely didn't turn out to be someone he could intimidate or scare away from Heaven. His plan had failed, and his hate for Heaven's involvement in a same-sex relationship with Jazz only irked and irritated him more.

Heaven could still very well see the fury on Breezy's face when he marched up to her apartment later that evening. He scowled, fumed, and barely uttered a word as he handed her a sheet of paper, neatly folded and bearing a stamp from the DC Superior Court on the lower left corner.

Heaven wasn't sure of what it was about until she read the heading.

It almost prompted laughter from her mouth, but she held it back out of respect for the man whose ego was already bruised.

Unknown to him, Jazz had called her immediately after she slapped the living shit out of him and duly narrated the course of events as they had occurred to her. It was funny as hell, and even while she felt irritated by Breezy's actions, she felt proud of Jazz for standing up to the man who definitely had no rule or right over her life.

"Is this all you got?" she asked in a snarky tone.

Breezy shot her a deep glare and replied. "Don't you fuck with me! Tell your fuck buddy she had better not be around me, or I am dragging her ass to jail for assaulting me."

Heaven finally let it all out; she laughed hard and wouldn't stop, even while Breezy's face didn't look so pleased.

"A lady slapped the shit out of you because you stalked and insulted her, and the next best move you could think of was to head over to get a restraining order?" she asked in mocking tone. "Your testosterone levels must be freaking high right now."

Breezy turned away and marched to his truck and sped off into the distance like a mad man. She couldn't help but feel glad to have seen his back just around the same time Jazz's truck pulled toward her house.

The sight warmed her heart, as was always the case. Jazz stepped out of the truck with some bags of brand new linens as she approached Heaven.

"Hey, sweetie!" She greeted Heaven from where she stood carrying the bags.

"I figured since I haven't had time to properly play with the little one and that I owe her so much for sharing her amazing mother with me, I decided to gift Hilly with brand new toddler furniture."

She coordinated the delivery and set-up of the rather exquisite bedroom setup for Heaven. It was bound to be expensive, no doubt, and Heaven had not expected it, considering she earned far much more than Jazz now in her new job. "You just missed Breezy." Heaven smirked before planting a kiss on Jazz's cheek.

Jazz frowned as she collected the restraining order from Heaven. "He can go fuck himself." Heaven chuckled and thanked Jazz with a warm kiss as they entered the house.

Soon their lips locked.

"I believe it's time you got acquainted with the little lady," Heaven said, hurrying over to the bedroom to get

Hilly. She soon returned with the bubbly girl in her arms. She handed Hilly over to Jazz, and surprisingly, even while Jazz had never had a child of her own, they seemed to hit it off.

Hilly laughed and giggled at Jazz, while the latter just could not contain her excitement, or even hold back how she felt. Heaven felt warm at heart; it felt beautiful just seeing how peaceful and loving everything was in that moment. It didn't even seem to matter that Breezy had threatened to ruin the mood earlier; that was far-gone and she didn't care a hoot about it.

"She is absolutely adorable," Jazz said. "I mean, I think I can spend hours with Hilly and not even feel tired or bored."

Heaven leaned close to the girls, and they shared the next hour together before Jazz offered to take them both out.

"It will be our first outing together, and I have to apologize for something, babe," Jazz said.

"What?" Heaven asked with a harmless frown.

"This outing is for the princess herself, and you aren't allowed to take the spotlight from her," Jazzy teased.

Heaven didn't care. She was happy she would at least get the chance to be out there with the duo. It was bound to be an excellent day.

"Lest I forget," Jazz said as they headed for the car, "I got her something else."

It was a brand-new Apple laptop; Heaven couldn't help but feel her lower jaw drop. She wrapped her arms around Jazz, planted her lips on hers once again and spent the next minute enjoying the affection that came with being with Jazz.

Chapter 15
Meet My Parent

Weary as hell and feeling her legs almost refuse to function appropriately, she glanced at her watch and noted the time. It was almost six in the evening, and the plan was to meet up with Jazz by six on the dot. The entire day had been used up searching for new single-family homes around Potomac, Maryland, after sourcing a proper real estate agent for the new home.

Getting a proper agent had been tough as hell, with many of them seeking out deals Heaven wasn't ready to take. She finally got an agent, and together, they checked listings, with an array of options. It was something of an overwhelming process for Heaven initially.

It was even more amazing she had arrived here, considering that she was one step away from living on the roadside had the Section 8 apartment not come through for her.

Now, she was capable of actually acquiring a house

after sorting her credit problems once and for all.

She had felt some beads of teardrops fall on either side of her face through those periods as they moved from one house to another to check them out.

"Babe! Babe!" Jazz's voice dragged Heaven back into consciousness.

She smiled and immediately casted aside her drowning thoughts.

"Please tell me someone is thinking about me." She smiled.

"Well, I was thinking about how my mother is bound to love you," Heaven replied with a wink.

Jazz gasped and seemed to have forgotten what their plan was.

"Shit!" Jazz muttered. "I totally forgot."

She took a look at the rather form-fitting pants she had on and seemed to grow bothered by the passing second about how things would turn out around Heaven's mother.

Heaven just could not help herself as she burst out laughing.

"Come on, girl, I'm almost having a meltdown here." Jazz frowned.

Heaven pulled her closer and locked her hand with Jazz's. "You are amazing, and I know this for a fact that my mother is going to love you."

Jazz wished so. She knew people were bound to have mixed opinions and expressions at their daughter being involved in a same-sex relationship.

"My mom will love you," Heaven reiterated. The reassuring words from Heaven's mouth seemed to be all Jazz needed in that moment.

Hours later, they were standing outside the door leading into Heaven's mother's house. Jazz was drenched not just in sweat but in ample nervousness as she tried to hide how she was feeling. Heaven locked hands with her lover, trying to comfort her as best as possible. The ride had been nerve-racking, and so much so that Heaven decided to take control of the wheel. "Just take in deep breaths, honey." Heaven encouraged Jazz, and she nodded her head tenderly and glued her focus on the door as it creaked open in what was beginning to feel like a wait that lasted forever.

Heaven thought she could hear Jazz's heart thump and stomp, while hers, too, had begun to mirror the anxious expression.

Heaven's mother stood between the doors and glanced at Heaven before slowly moving her eyes to Jazz. "You must be Jazz." Those words were nothing short of draining, and Jazz stuttered to respond as Heaven's mother's face bore no expression whatsoever. The bland appearance was good enough to confuse anyone and make them believe there was a problem somewhere. Heaven's mother suddenly switched. "Don't just stand there like a log of wood, come on in and give me a warm hug!" Jazz let off a huge sigh of relief as she wiped her forehead clear of sweat. She wrapped her arms around Heaven's mother and listened to the woman mention some really sweet words into her ear. "You have nothing to be scared about," she said. "I have been waiting for the two of you, and I sure as hell wanted to meet the lady responsible for my daughter's smile." Heaven walked into the house last, locked the door behind her, and watched her lover and her mother immediately hit it off.

They looked as though they had been friends for a very long time. With the wonderful aroma filling the entire house, Heaven knew her mother was well prepared to receive them.

"These look delicious," Jazz said as she took her seat by Heaven's mother.

"Well, I couldn't make a shabby meal for my baby's lover, now, could I?" Heaven's mom replied.

The support, which was ever present, was the reason Heaven loved her mother without a doubt. Her mother, forever a backbone and a pillar of support, spent the night getting to know Jazz and even pleading for the two girls to sleep over in the extra room until morning. Jazz would oblige, meaning Heaven had no choice.

Never had Heaven thought of having another lady other than Michell (her ex BFF) in her mother's house, much less of one she would be indulging in sexual activities.

Morning came sooner than they had anticipated. Heaven and Jazz bade her mother farewell and drove off together, with Jazz still feeling rather sleepy as they distanced themselves from the house where they had spent their night.

"That was fun," Jazz said.

Heaven turned briefly to look at her. "Yeah. My mom really took a liking to you."

Jazz shook her head abruptly. She had other things in mind when she spoke.

"I mean spending the night under a roof with you. It always comes with the feeling that things can really work, and I want more," Jazz replied. "I want stability and more, without having to return to my house late at night or in the early hours of the morning."

Heaven screeched the car to a halt as she realized what Jazz seemed to be talking about.

"Are you serious?' Heaven asked.

Jazz cocked her head in affirmation.

"You really want to live with me?" Heaven asked to be sure.

Jazz cocked her head once again, affirming every single word she had uttered.

"But…but," Heaven stammered.

"I love you, and I believe we can be happier living under the same roof," Jazz explained. "I really think it makes things better, and we both can even find ourselves doing more together."

Heaven had no idea about how to respond, but glad that she had her mind focused on moving into a single family home already.

It meant she was moving out of her Section 8 housing for good and moving into a proper house with the woman she loved.

"I need to work through the process," Heaven replied. "I have to apply for a loan, and ensure all outstanding debt is cleared first, and…"

Jazz reached out to Heaven, leaned closer, and planted a peck on her cheek. "We will figure it out."

Monday

Heaven would indeed figure it out when she got off work. After getting permission to head off earlier than usual, she sought out means to clear her credit card debt. The process turned out to be much more tiring and draining than she had expected, but driven by the will and desire to come out on top, she saw it through.

Chapter 16

Moving on Up. It's Been Great, Section 8!

Heaven was jittery as she attempted to open her email. She figured it couldn't be worse than being told she didn't qualify for the loan she applied for, but the thought of remaining in her Section 8 apartment continued to haunt her.

She had definitely outgrown it, and her income exceeded the guidelines and her current situation meant she ought to be leaving soon enough. Besides, Heaven's plan worked flawlessly – Section 8 was meant to be a bridge, not the final solution.

Jazz rushed into the room as though she had been worried sick something terrible was going on with Heaven. Her eyes bore absolute concern, and as she walked through the door, Heaven felt her heart beat aloud and disturbingly too. Worrying about loan approvals was hard, and while she stared into Jazz's eyes, it was obvious Jazz shared in her worries as well.

"It can only go two ways, Heaven." Jazz tried to

sound encouraging. "If they don't approve, we can try to get another one, and reapply for it until you get what you want." It sounded easier than Heaven had assumed, and the longer Heaven thought about it, the more difficult it felt for her to actually open the email from the bank. "How about we check it together?" Jazz asked. Heaven had not thought of it, but the feeling of having Jazz's hand on computer's mouse seemed to help lessen the burden on herself.

Together, the ladies clicked the email and read the communication therein.

Slowly and nervously, they moved their heads from left to right and then back again until they finally got to the bottom of the email. It wasn't much to read, but they seemed to have read it more than once and continued to do so three times.

"They approved my loan request!" Heaven bellowed. "They approved my home loan!"

The joyful sound resonated through the entire house, and they jollied and screamed without ceasing.

"I will give you the deposit or whatever you need for your new house!" Jazz said.

"I want to be a part of this, and I would like to help in any way that I can."

Heaven shook her head. The loan was bound to be a substantial one, and she didn't want to continue to impose on Jazz, which was what she felt already, considering the gifts Jazz had gotten Hilly and how much she was doing. Heaven wanted to do her best to bear a good portion of the financial weight.

"You really shouldn't bother yourself," Heaven said.

Jazz waved her words away. "We are definitely celebrating this, and we are doing it in style." Jazz dragged Heaven up from her seat and led her to the car immediately. Heaven put on Hilly's sweater and placed her on her hip.

"Where are we headed?" Heaven asked.

"To the mall," Jazz replied. "My queen deserves some really gorgeous outfits and jewels."

Hearing those words caused Heaven to blush as she shook her head and imagined how sweeter life was bound to be for her, with Jazz invested in her ordeals. She barely remembered Breezy and his drama. In fact, nothing about him would pop through her mind while they shopped for the most glamorous Louis Vuitton handbags and shoes, and products from other designers she wanted. Jazz spoiled Heaven, and Heaven recalled the days when all she wanted was to be loved and spoiled, just a little.

All Jazz demanded was for Heaven to make a wish, and they would be granted it immediately. Jazz turned to Heaven as they were almost done shopping. "What happens with the Section 8 housing?" Heaven shrugged her shoulders and replied. "I'm writing my letter first thing tomorrow morning. "I will have sixty days to get out."

It had always been Heaven's plan to visit the DC Housing Authority to inform them of her plans to move out.

Watching it materialize was a dream come true.

"Well, we'd better meet with the real estate agent and

put a contract on the house tomorrow for the house in Potomac, then," Jazz said.

Their plans were in sync, and that was exactly what they were bound to do the following day.

Heaven was on the rise, and nothing was about to stop her love of Jazz, their plan to get a home together, build a life together, and her long dream to move out of Section 8.

After all, Heaven's income overqualified her for the housing program, and it was time to allow another mom the opportunity to use the housing program as a stepping-stone to future goals.

Everything felt perfect in that very moment.

Chapter 17
Climbing Higher

Her gaze peered through the glass and stretched farther from her office as endless thoughts ran through her mind without end. She smiled, smirked, and oftentimes let out a huge sigh of what felt like relief, knowing too well that she had somehow and some way succeeded in actually getting to where she was through hard work.

Yet there was something more to how she was feeling in that moment, and it had to do with the sweet brunette princess she had woken up in bed with that morning. Nothing had felt so perfect for Heaven. In fact, she had never thought of enjoying such wonderful period of time in her life without hassles. It was made sweeter by the fact that it seemed her haters and enemies were being tossed out of her life one at a time.

Wislou was far-gone. Being able to even oust the stubborn woman many regarded to be as tough as a roach from the office was deemed a godly act.

It had also earned her a cult-like status within the walls of her workplace.

Even more, her actions, deeds, and work ethic had gained her more positive recognition. In that moment, while Heaven remained in her seat with her back to the door, she reminisced about it all. She had not really had time to think it all through, but there she was, amassing everything and ensuring she played them step-by-step through her mind so she wasn't about to miss anything at all. Life had slowly morphed, transformed from one of uncertainty, lack, and measures of suffering and anguish into a sweeter feeling and a great deal of fulfillment. She wasn't anywhere near where she wanted to be, but there was growth and that in itself was the purpose to life.

"How time flies," she murmured to herself, spinning in her chair like a child who was just granted a new toy.

The day was beautiful and had been that way from the moment she parted her eyes that morning. She had assumed the night before was more beautiful, but waking up to the sight right before her and by her side in bed had proven her wrong. Waking up to find Jazz in bed, sleeping like a baby, with those absolutely gorgeous eyes slowly wakening to stare at her had caused Heaven's heart to skip in beats. It had caused her to draw closer, wrap her arms around her lover, and wished she didn't have to leave the bed for any reason whatsoever. Unfortunately, there was work to be done, and even when they said their good-byes that morning, she could still very well taste Jazz's lips on hers, smell her scent all over her body.

The smile on Hilly's face was absolutely wonderful. The triangle felt perfect, and Heaven was glad it wasn't as distorted as it used to feel when it was just Breezy and Hilly she had in the picture.

Jazz, she thought as she spun around some more.

Missing her woman, Heaven reached for her cell phone and dialed Jazz's contact immediately. Work still had not commenced that morning, and Heaven had enough time on her hands. She could feel her breath heighten and some measure of anxiety slowly begin to trickle down her spine as she held the phone to her ear.

Everything about speaking with Jazz often made her feel like a child and that morning was no different.

"Jazz, where are you?" Heaven said to herself without realizing she had spoken out loud.

"Probably hung up on work, as you ought to be right about now," someone replied, oddly close to Heaven.

Heaven, startled, ended the call and turned her chair around to look at the blank-faced Mr. Greenstein.

The man barely wore a smile and held his hands before him, as his eyes remained fixated on her. Heaven adjusted in her seat and managed a harmless smile.

"Good morning, sir." She finally managed to reply after being caught off guard.

He slowly walked to the seat before her, pulled it back, and slowly helped himself into it. He looked paler than usual and obviously not as bright in the face as he used to be.

"Is everything all right?" Heaven asked, knowing the man who was often too busy for even himself wouldn't be in her office if something wasn't up.

Mr. Greenstein replied. "These past few months have been nothing short of remarkable, haven't they?"

Heaven nodded her head. She had won a lot more than she had lost, and it just could not be cast aside.

"Well, I am here because I want more," he said. The ambiguous words caused Heaven to tilt her head to the side while she awaited some better explanation.

"I want more from you and more for you.

It means the next few months, you and I will be working closely together -- I will be taking you under my wing."

Heaven felt a twitch in her belly as her eyes widened and her mouth slowly parted.

"That… that…" she stammered, unsure of how best to respond.

He finally let off a smile before slowly getting on his feet and unbuttoning his jacket.

"I need you to show me and everyone in here that you have what it takes to be more," he said. "A whole lot of things are counting on whatever energy you give to me."

Heaven shot to her feet and replied as boldly as she could. "I promise you I'll give nothing but my best, sir." Mr. Greenstein nodded, turned away with a smile, and whistled as he exited her office. Heaven remained standing, too paralyzed to even move as she wondered what had just occurred. She was about to work directly under one of the most powerful men around her. He had chosen her, of all people. Her heart could barely contain the joy she felt as her cell phone rang, with the caller being Jazz.

Two months had passed since Heaven got that fateful visit from Mr. Greenstein, and the effect of that meeting was still being felt on that early Monday morning.

She rushed down the hallway, knowing well that Mr. Greenstein was counting on her to sort some issues related to the HR department. He had called to say he was coming in late and told Heaven he trusted in her to handle things appropriately.

She rushed through her office door, slammed her files on the table, and stopped to notice an envelope with the office stamp at the lower right corner. Heaven looked around, unsure of how anyone could have actually gotten into her office.

Since the events with Wislou, she had ensured her office doors would remain closed and that her things were guarded properly, with nobody having access to her workspace unless she deemed it so.

Somewhat nervous and with trembling hands, she picked up the envelope as a note fell through from underneath it. Heaven picked it up and read the handwritten note with some sense of familiarity. The handwriting was without doubt from Mr. Greenstein. The oddity in the affair caused Heaven to pull up a chair before attempting to open the sealed envelope. She looked around a bit, unsure of what to make of the situation, before tearing through the envelope and locking her eyes on the note she had picked earlier.

"For everything you have been…this is the least I can do and I sincerely hope you continue to prove me right… Greenstein"

Heaven immediately placed the note to the side and read through the letter inside the envelope. She gasped and felt her lungs almost collapse as she stared at the official letter with trembling hands.

"No," Heaven said more than once without actually taking note. "No!" Her shriek definitely alerted passersby as they stole glances at the elated woman inside her office. She could not believe her eyes at all. "He recommended me," she whispered before shooting up from her seat.

"He fucking recommended me!"

It was all she could say as she danced around the room in hysteria. They had worked together in various aspects of the human resources department, and he had ensured she learned policies, protocols and training techniques, which she used to onboard newly hired federal employees.

Heaven couldn't believe her eyes, but she soon began to realize that every single project and every single exercise he had been putting her through was to ensure she learned enough to gain the promotion he had just given to her.

"I got promoted to GS-14!" she cried at the top of her voice while her hips swayed with the happiest dance skill she had ever shown. Her salary had finally reached six figures.

During her moment of happiness, Heaven heard something pop up on her computer, indicating she had just gotten an instant message via Facebook.

Still elated and beyond words, she hoped it was Jazz so she could share the good news with her lover. She raced over to the computer, clicked to Facebook and realized it had been sent from an unknown source. In the message was a link, and without thinking much about it, Heaven clicked and watched the screen burst open to the sight of her former best friend, Michell, flaunting a protruded belly on Facebook.

What in the hell? Heaven thought. She never knew Michell to be one with interest in becoming a mother, and seeing her with a bulging belly looked absolutely odd, to say the least. She shook her head, decided not to care about whatever was going on with Michell, and focused on her win in that moment. Yet there was something about the Facebook message that caused Heaven some measure of concern.

"I cannot wait to have my mixed baby," Michell had typed underneath the post.

You're having a mixed-race baby? Heaven thought before attempting to close the page. No sooner had she closed the page that she saw another attachment underneath the video. Whoever had sent the message was definitely on the verge of telling her something that would attempt to ruin the wonderful day she was having.

"What's this?" Heaven asked herself as she clicked on the added attachment. She felt her promotion letter in her hand drop, her lower jaw drop, and her eyes immediately flood with tears and disbelief at the same time.

"What the fuck?" she muttered.

Fuming red, unsure of what to say, she paced in the parking lot and waited for his dingy truck to pull over. She figured there was no use trying to talk on the phone—they needed to be face-to-face, and she was right. Heaven had found it even harder to keep the information to herself, considering she read through the words and watched the video the anonymous tipper sent over and over and again until she could not take it any longer. Breezy's truck pulled into the parking lot, and he stepped out with the usual smug look on his face.

He mouthed off almost immediately. "This had better be you trying to come back to your senses and apologize after the stunt you pulled with that trick bitch you've been sleeping with."

Heaven shook her head in disbelief of his self-righteousness. He was even more irritating to deal with after getting her promotion, only to have it soiled by Breezy again, as he always attempted to do when something good came her way.

"Well, how is your trick doing?" Heaven struck out immediately. "Don't you find it hypocritical to be smashing that traitor I called a friend and then go on to get her pregnant when you and I have a baby?" Breezy seemed to lose his strength and composure almost immediately.

He ran his fingers through his hair and bit his lower lip, without being unsure of how best to respond.

"Heaven," he muttered. "Shit!'

Heaven shook her head and seconded his word. "Shit! You fucked Michell?

You got that hoe pregnant, while you were still trying to get in my panties?"

Breezy looked destabilized. He parted his lips countless times, stuttering almost every time he attempted to speak, before finally falling to his knees.

"I was being foolish." He succumbed to taking blame for his deeds. "She was all over me, and I just fell."

Heaven could not believe the latter part of his sentence. "What exactly happened? You just fucking tripped and fell into her pussy?"

Breezy got to his feet again, trying to reach out to her, but Heaven shoved his hands away.

She had had enough of him and every drama that came with associating herself with him.

"Of all people in the world to fuck, you fucking chose

Michell," Heaven muttered in disappointment. "I want nothing to do with you."

Breezy tugged at her dress and prompted Heaven to stop.

"I swear to you, I didn't do anything with her again after that fucking video you saw on my phone," he said. "That was the only time, and we split up."

Heaven's head rang wild as she tried to recall every single person she had seen in the video all over again. One lady remained unknown, and she had not quite been able to put a face to the frame because she always seemed to hide away from the camera.

"That was Michell in the fucking sex tape?" Heaven asked.

Breezy, now knowing he was caught and that there was absolutely nothing he could do, reluctantly bobbed his head. "I never saw her again" he said again, while Heaven knew he was lying through his teeth, as usual.

She felt the sting of betrayal ravage every nerve in her body as Breezy fell to his knees in plea. She shrugged his hands off of her and held her breath for a moment before finally knowing what to say. "This is the last time you'll have anything to do with me or anyone in my life whom I care about," she assured him in a bold tone. "See you in court." She shoved him away, walked off without looking back, and for the first time in a while, she felt free and absolutely vindicated. The relief was satisfying, and she definitely felt lighter.

Heaven hoped to go home, shower, and call Jazz to come over.

They still needed to celebrate the fact that Mr. Greenstein had signed the official papers and recommended her for the promotion she had gotten that week.

Chapter 18

Oh No! Not Mr. Greenstein

Heaven glanced at her watch for the umpteenth time and soon realized it was just like the day before and the day before then. Mr. Greenstein, ever so punctual in the workplace, had not shown up for work over the past week, and it was becoming disturbing. There had been rumors about the man being ill, but nothing was confirmed.

Heaven had planned on thanking him in person that morning for everything he had done, when he was due to come back after taking a week off from work.

Tired of waiting and with a court hearing with Breezy in the afternoon, she walked over to speak with his secretary.

Dana Sandoval, Mr. Greenstein's trusted secretary and Heaven's very close friend, was standing by the door with her face buried in a handkerchief as Heaven drew closer.

The sight was definitely not a warm one, and it prompted Heaven to stop for a moment before continuing her walk until she arrived before the obviously distraught woman. Dana sniffed when she saw Heaven and wrapped her arms around the confused latter. "I am so sorry, Heaven. I am so sorry."

Heaven slowly pulled away. "What is going on?" Dana motioned to speak, but every time she attempted to, wails eased past her mouth and endless cries filled the air.

"He is dead," she whispered amid sniffs and tears. "Mr. Greenstein passed away this morning." Heaven's entire world felt like it had just clattered hard to the ground and shattered into a zillion pieces. She let go of Dana and slowly stepped backward, her lips trembling and every part of her body in denial of the information she had just been given. Mr. Greenstein had done everything within his power to raise her through the ranks and place her comfortably where she was. His immaculate trainings and mentorship were better than anything Heaven had gone through in her professional life. While she stood by the door, staring into his empty office, her heart broke further. "This cannot be happening," she muttered. "This cannot be fucking happening!"

Dana tried to console her, but to no avail. Heaven was heartbroken and lost, and there was just no telling what she would do next. It was obvious there was nothing about the work environment that would excite her anymore.

She was definitely not going to fancy being in the workspace where her favorite person and mentor once existed without him.

Dana tugged at Heaven's arm and whispered, "He didn't want anyone to know, and even I had no idea about how serious his health issues were until now." Heaven cocked her head and faked a smile. "I cannot do this right now. I cannot continue here without him," Heaven confessed. Dana acknowledged her words with a nod and watched Heaven race off to the restroom to cry her eyes out. She didn't want to be consoled, and she definitely didn't want to continue work there, either. She immediately sought a transfer out of Mr. Greenstein's office.

Three weeks had passed since Mr. Greenstein passed away, and everything seemed to continue to follow a rather distressing pattern. One glimmer of light in the dark period was the fact that Breezy had not shown up for the court hearing, and automatically had his case against Jazz thrown out, while his claim to Hilly was equally dismissed.

It was the only glimmer of hope for Heaven while she sat in a completely foreign office that morning, taking in subtle breaths and hoping her interviewer had not or was not noticing how nervous and distressed she was.

It had taken her just a week to decide against working in her previous workplace.

People thought she was crazy when she told them she was transferring and packing her things, but it was something Jazz had stood by her on before she decided to make the decision. Yet, just as always, Mr. Greenstein had come through, as his secretary, Dana, Heaven's friend, hooked her up with a new job listing in an affiliate office.

"You should check it out," Dana had said on that morning before Heaven exited the building. "I worked there for a while before being temporarily transferred here to work with Mr. Greenstein." The trust and belief Heaven had in Dana was the only reason she had decided to take the opportunity to interview and why she was in that seat on that morning.

The morning of the interview

The interviewer cleared his throat once again and glanced at Heaven. "You have come a long way, Miss Davis, and your resume is remarkable." Heaven nodded subtly. "I must confess your training and the amount of work you put into your previous office is beyond anything I have from other applicants, but for some reason, I still don't get the enthusiasm from you," John Rattlecliff said as he leaned back in his seat.

"We need people who are serious about getting this job and who are willing to show us just how serious they are and can be." Heaven sighed and felt drained as she got to her feet and headed for the door. The truth was, she still wasn't mentally fit to handle anything before her. Getting to the door, hand on the doorknob, she paused and turned around. "I lost someone dear to me and who mentored me in my last place of work. If it wasn't for Mr. Greenstein, I doubt anything in the resume you have before you would be possible. I am truly sorry for being lackadaisical. Perhaps I should have delayed seeking a transfer." Mr. Rattlecliff stood up from his seat and replied. "Mr. Greenstein? The late Mr. Greenstein?"

Heaven nodded her head and sighed.

"I was a former employee of his, and he was good to me in ways nobody ever was. In fact, I got this job because he recommended me." He motioned for Heaven to return to her seat, and they shared wonderful memories and recollections of the man before his passing.

Mr. Rattlecliff paused for a moment as he rubbed his chin. "Considering how good your resume is, how highly recommended you come, and the fact I always devote myself to assisting those Mr. Greenstein has taken under his wing, you have the job." He turned to his computer and composed an email to informing HR that the transferred was approved and with that transfer came a temporary promotion to a GS-15.

"Congratulations on achieving a temporary GS-15, which is the highest possible level anyone can partake in while they work for the US government," he said with a smile and an extended arm.

Heaven felt herself freeze for a moment before slowly meeting his hand with hers halfway across the table.

Outside the building, Jazz looked nervous as she stepped out of her car for the umpteenth time. She glanced at her watch endlessly and continued to do so until she saw a straight-faced Heaven step out of the building. "Babe," Heaven said in a tender tone.

"Please tell me you got the job," Jazz pleaded in a nervous tone.

Heaven approached her, wrapped her arms around Jazz's waist, and leaned closer to lock her lips with Jazz's.

"Looks like you and I are going to definitely buying our new home," Heaven whispered. Jazz couldn't agree more as the duo headed to the car. Hilly smiled at her mother as the two ladies got into the car. "Hey, baby girl, how do you feel about the three of us moving into our new home together?" Heaven said to her baby as she picked her up from the backseat. With Jazz owning a home in Washington, DC also, Heaven felt even more jived up about securing her own future too. Jazz planned to keep her home and rent it out to college students from Howard University. Jazz stole a glance at her love as she drove. "When do we finally get to move in as a family?" It would happen three weeks later.

The trio, Heaven, Hilly, and Jazz, would move into their new home in Potomac, MD.

Chapter 19

Catastrophic Tragedy Rips Heaven to Pieces

Jazz had come through as she had assured, and Heaven just could not believe her eyes. It had been a year since she began at her new workplace, and everything seemed to have been going on perfectly until some weeks ago when Heaven felt the need for more.

She was working in a place many would die for, and she was fixed for life where she was, but she wasn't one who ever wanted to settle for less. That was precisely what she was doing.

To make things worse, she had an envious supervisor who constantly found ways to hammer how jealous she was of Heaven by demanding the most outrageous work deeds.

Yet Heaven soldiered through, knowing she had Jazz's love and Hilly by her side to help her through the process. Jazz had even managed to put up with her endless nagging and complaints while they were at home together. Her current job was somewhat draining. It did pay her well and provided the benefits she needed, with growth on several platforms of her life, but it still didn't bring the kind of fulfillment she craved.

It definitely didn't come through with the self-growth she wanted, and it didn't help to have an egotistic supervisor watching her every move. It was why this particular morning was nothing short of mesmerizing and beautiful. Heaven sat in what was meant to be a lunch meeting with Jazz, and found herself with three other people she could tell were of great importance to her woman. It made her nerves stiffen with anxiety for a bit, but watching Jazz smirk from where she was only reassured her of the fact that there would be nothing to worry about.

"What is going on?" Heaven asked as she glanced at her watch, realizing she ought to be back in the office in about an hour.

Jazz walked over, planted herself in the empty seat next to Jazz and replied. "You know those problems and plans you constantly rattle my ears with every time you come back from work?"

Heaven nodded. "Yes." Jazz held out her hand and pointed to the trio before them. "Meet my personal accountant, my business advisor, and my strategist." Heaven still wasn't sure of what her lover wanted, but she could sense some of it already.

"I need you to pitch your ideas on Glamour Girls Travel, just as you ring it into my ears every single day, but to them," Jazz explained.

Heaven could not believe her eyes or her ears. Being granted access to the trio before her was definitely a needed step toward establishing her desired company. It was something she had thought of for months, with no means of ease. Jazz had listened to every bit of the plan, and while she sat there, grinning from ear to ear, she was glad at heart that Heaven could now do the same to professionals who were definitely going to help her. Heaven called her office without caring about how late she was going to be.

She riddled the three before her about her ideas, and within half an hour, they were already strategizing on business plans and how to make her dream come to life.

"Registering your brand name as Glamour Girls Travel, LLC is something we can easily get going for you, but we need to speak about the financial implications and costs as well," Jazz's accountant noted. Heaven had dreaded that aspect, and the more she thought of it, the more baffled and worried she was. It was a major stumbling block for her, and one of the reasons she had not attempted to go on with the plans to open her own business for some time. Her salary was good, but it still wasn't ever going to be enough to get things sorted. "Well." Heaven paused without being sure of what words to use next.

"Well, we have that covered," Jazz added about the finances.

"We do?" Heaven asked as she turned her head to the left to shoot Jazz a curious look. "How?"

Jazz snickered oddly, sat up in her seat, and said, "My

smoothie company will be funding the entire business with no interest. Since we are in this together, I figure it is something we both need to work on whichever way we can." Heaven looked dumbfounded and unsure of what to do. She shifted in her seat, ground her teeth in nervousness, before jumping up and wrapping her arms around her love. They shared a warm kiss before returning to discuss how the business would be set up and what it would entail.

Heaven was soon about to realize how much her dream meant to her partner and how fast things could go if one truly had the **right backing and support**.

Jazz had also enlisted her personal website developer to assist in making the business into what Heaven dreamed it would be. "What are we looking at in this business of yours? What exactly do you want to convey to your c potential customers regarding Glamour Girls Travel?" her strategist asked.

"We will be focusing on adding glam to products which include travel apparel, luggage, beach towels and accessories inspired by exquisite taste and affordability to willing consumer." Heaven explained.

It was as easy and simple as that.

A month later

Heaven had just gotten off her phone as the latest developments on the orders her company Glamour Girls

Travel, LLC had just received. Business was definitely on the up, and in ways she had never even imagined. She stared at the phone in her hand, smiled endlessly, and sighed in relief before clocking in her last work project for the day in hopes of heading out for dinner with Jazz. Working in her office had come with ease ever since she had an outlet for her frustration though her business.

Jazz had been super supportive too, consistently investing in the business without the will or intent of receiving anything in return. Heaven couldn't have asked for a better start to her business.

"Five hundred freaking orders today alone." She chuckled as she scrolled through the listings sent to her on her phone. She forwarded them through to those she had hired to help make the procedures quite easier. Since her online presence was just growing, she still had a lot to do on ground before actually gaining better followership. No sooner had she sent through the order requests did she hear her phone beep and see a strange number calling. Unfazed by the call, she lifted the phone to her ear and felt her entire mood dampen almost immediately.

"Where is she?" Heaven asked. She took note of the address the stranger had mentioned to her, tucked her phone into her pocket, left her job and hailed a cab immediately.

"This cannot be happening," she muttered to herself.

The information she had just received was damning and disturbing; her mother was in the hospital for reasons she still had no idea about. The caller had not said anything other than the need for her to come immediately. Heaven prayed her heart out while she was in the cab. She could feel sweat running down every part of her body as she wished there was a faster route to their destination. They finally arrived after what felt like the longest journey of her life. She raced out of the cab after paying without receiving her change and burst through the hospital's front door like a gladiator in search of an opponent. It was her first time in that hospital, but it was the closest to her mother's workplace and understandably the one they had to bring her to.

"My mother was brought her moments ago!" Heaven shouted as she walked over to the receptionist. She tendered her mother's name and description, before watching the lady at the reception wear a saddened expression on her face. "Please, come with me," she said as she led Heaven down the hallway. Heaven's heart threatened to leave her chest, and her knees definitely wanted to fail her. She looked around the wards they passed, but no signs of her mother were there until they arrived at the end of the hallway, just one ward left.

A doctor stood by the door, wearing a blank expression as he gave orders to the nurses by his side. The receptionist introduced Heaven to the doctor, and Heaven could very well tell something was wrong. The door to the room was closed, the window slits shut, and the doctor stood in the doorway, trying to prevent her from going in immediately.

"Your mother was rushed here on suspicions of a stroke, and we proffered every possible medical assistance we could give to her, but we lost her," the doctor explained. Heaven shoved him to the side and barged into the room in hopes it was some sick joke. She rushed into the room and stopped some feet by her mother's bed, with her mom's lifeless body right before her. Everything fell into deafening silence and everything felt numb for Heaven almost immediately.

She held her breath, hoped to wake up from whatever harrowing dream she was having, and see her mom's smiling face beckoning her to come, but to no avail.

The reality of her mother transitioning only struck her when she called out to her mother , but got no response still. "Oh my God! Oh my God! Oh my God!" Heaven bellowed in pain as she fell to her knees. She couldn't bear the thought of touching her mother, seeing she wasn't going to respond. Her entire world felt like a wall of dominos crumbling down all at once.

The nightmares didn't end, and even while she had taken a leave of absence from work, Heaven still could not get over the fact that she had lost one of the three persons alive who ever truly loved her, her mother.

With her vision blurry from the countless number of pills she had ingested, which seemed like they were taking too long to do the trick, she armed herself with a kitchen knife and staggered toward the bathroom. It was just days since the harrowing news had gotten to her. The days had felt like months, and even while Jazz had been supportive, it still wasn't enough. Heaven wanted her mother back.

Feeling dejected and tired of the haunting pain she felt at heart and the immense emotional torture she slipped into the bathtub, filled it up with water, and slowly slit her left wrist. The writhing pain did nothing to deter her from doing the same to her right wrist as well. She could feel blood slowly begin to trickle out as her breath heightened momentarily and then slumped. She looked up toward the sky, ready to meet her mother. Heaven stared at the bulb in the ceiling, feeling herself slowly drift in and out of consciousness as her vision soon grew blurrier by the passing second.

Wheezing softly, unsure of what was going on around her anymore other than the pain that she had lost the most important person in her life. Heaven slipped off into slumber and hoped it would be permanent.

She simply wanted to die.

At the hospital

"I think she's coming out of it," Jazz said, sounding as optimistic as ever. Yet, the problem with being so optimistic was the fact that Heaven had proved her wrong about three times already.

Breezy stood wide-eyed as he gawked at her as deeply as possible, hands on his waist and his demeanor obviously distressed. He had been on suicide watch for the past three days with Jazz, and they still could not trust Heaven not to drift back into her suicidal state.

"I never want to have to see her the way I did some days back," Breezy had said to Jazz countless time through their suicide watch.

He had found her lying in her pool of blood and barely breathing.

Having come over, as it was his day to be in charge of Hilly, the front door had been left ajar and he walked in and found her almost dead and called an ambulance to rush her to the hospital, where they stabilized her before sending her to the psychiatric unit. It was now 5 days since Heaven tried to kill herself, and even while she opened her eyes and struggled to sit in upright, she still wasn't with them. She just couldn't pull herself out of it, no matter how hard she tried.

"Heaven? Darling?" Jazz called out, hoping and trying to reach Heaven.

Heaven simply continued to stare blankly into the distance. "We need to speak about the funeral," Breezy whispered, but Jazz shook her head and warned him against saying anything that would set her off. "I will pay for everything. I'll take care of whatever expenses the funeral demands," Jazz promised.

The two simply stood and watched Heaven remain blank for a very long time, before finally turning her head to look at them. "She is gone. Mom is gone, and I can never see her again." Breezy scratched his head and stepped forward. "Well, there is a way you can interact with her." Jazz fumed and felt like yanking at Breezy's head. "You can enlist the assistance of a light worker to serve as a medium for you to speak with your mom," he continued.

Jazz fumed. "Are you nuts! She doesn't want that!"

Heaven finally spoke. "I actually do." Jazz sighed, realizing she wasn't going to win the fight, she nodded her head to agree. "On one condition," she suddenly said. "If we do this, you will continue with psychiatric therapy until you have recovered fully." Heaven sought to protest the deal, but she dearly wanted to interact with her mother through a medium. Heaven was desperate and willing to do anything to connect with her mom again.

"Please? Do it for Hilly," Breezy said as he stepped closer. "Hilly needs her mother, and you cannot leave her now."

Heaven lowered her head into her thighs and wept bitterly for the first time since she attempted to take her life. The scars on her wrists still hurt like hell but not as much as the ones on her heart. She couldn't quite imagine what sort of life Hilly would have gotten had she actually killed herself. "Okay," Heaven agreed subtly. "I will continue therapy." Jazz sighed in relief, knowing it was the best thing for the woman she dearly loved. "Thank you," she whispered to Heaven before drawing closer to kiss her. Breezy turned away and refused to look, still obviously troubled by the relationship between them, but without being able to do anything to stop the burning flames of love.

Four Months Later

Jazz sat on the other side of the table, watching the woman she so dearly loved toggling through her cell phone without acknowledging her presence for the past fifteen minutes. It was rapidly becoming the norm with Heaven, and Jazz was learning to go with it, for now at least, until she found the healing she needed.

Jazz finally cleared her throat in bid to gain the attention she needed. "Should I leave?" It was part of the healing process to have people from her life outside coming to visit her in the psychiatric facility until she was ready and deemed fit to live by herself and continue her life at large. "How are they taking your leave at work?" Jazz asked. Heaven finally dropped her cell phone and smiled. "It is extended leave, and everyone wants me to get better, so I'd say somewhat well."

Heaven was allowed to spend the week at home and returned to the facility on weekends; it still felt hard for the couple.

"I was told by your nurse that you've been drowning yourself in your Glam Travel business," Jazz said.

"Looks like things are really progressing, and I must say I am proud of you."

Heaven gets released from the psychiatric facility

Jazz was right as rain. Heaven had spent the past few months while on extended leave enhancing her business in ways she never thought possible.

Heaven emerged from a place of despair with a vengeance and a new focus and purpose in life.

Through the use of every marketing social media site and app, she had been able to promote her business, Glamour Girls Travel, LLC across the country, and orders were piling up to the point she was forced to hire more people to work for her. Jazz was able to hire the new employees for Heaven.

"I guess it is all I can do right now – focusing on this is therapy," Heaven replied before picking up her phone again. Jazz reached across the table to hold her hand while they locked gaze for a while. Heaven let off a huge sigh and shook her head.

"You have five people working under you within the space of four months," Jazz reminded her. "Your business is definitely thriving, and my guys even told me they weren't expecting anything close to this."

While they spoke and chattered on some more, Heaven's phone buzzed and Jazz smirked as she permitted her to pick it up. The look on Heaven's face was priceless, and it looked as though she was on the verge of fainting. "Oh my!" she screamed at the top of her voice and jumped up from her seat.

Jazz, startled, asked, "What is going on?" Heaven walked around the table and held out her phone to show the email she had just received. It was one from Rayana Pam, the first and only African-American airline owner in the country.

It was the cream atop her effort for the past few months using social media to attract celebrities and their friends who fancied glamorous travel accessories and apparel. "That…that…that's Rayana Pam," Jazz stammered. "She is fucking huge."

Heaven cocked her head as they read the email together.

The wealthy woman wanted Heaven to deliver some of her favorite glamour beach towels for use in one of her private jets and possibly her airplanes. "She wants Glamour Girls beach towels." Heaven snickered as she found it impossible to keep herself in check. She fisted the air, danced across the room, and Jazz soon joined her. "Get the order fulfilled promptly," Jazz encouraged her. Heaven did as she was told, almost out of breath and not knowing just how that one order from the millionaire was about to transform not just Glamour Girls Travel, LLC, but Heaven's life as well, forever.

Heaven turned to look at Jazz after sending the order

to her team. "I know you've been there for me every step of the way without asking for a single thing in return, and I cannot thank you enough." Jazz chuckled. "Well, when the celebrities come rushing over, don't forget this cute ass loves you."

One week later Rayana Pam posted a picture of her glamorous beach towel via Instagram and she tagged Heaven's social media handle in the post. Within minutes, Heaven and her business name tore through the internet, becoming the sensation and trending topic for the day. That one act not only gained her hundreds of new followers, but also brought in many more customers and more high-end clients than she could have ever imagined. Her ceaseless efforts were finally beginning to pay off. There seemed to be some light at the end of her tunnel, after all.

Chapter 20

Heaven Takes It ALL the Way to the Top

"I do" were the words that capped the beautiful afternoon.

They resonated with the wind and continued to travel afar toward the roaring ocean and soaring breeze that had born witness to the beautiful event.

The sky was heavenly blue, and the weather was just perfect for what Heaven would term to be the best day of her life. She had stood there, wondering about everything she had gone through in the past.

It was just months since she attempted to take her own life, but there she was, on the verge of beginning life afresh, and not by herself but with the two most important people in her life.

With her bare feet buried in the sand, the most beautiful flowers surrounding them in a heart shape and the bashing sound and waves from the ocean constantly reminding them of where they were, Heaven seized Jazz's hands and held them firmly in hers. "I love you, and I always want to be married to you," she said. The vows they just shared in their subtle-themed wedding wasn't enough. Heaven wasn't sure anything would be enough, no matter how much she said or how much she was willing to show Jazz. Together they had grown love and sustained it in a way Heaven never could have imagined. Together, they paddled through the difficult times, and Jazz never once left her side.

While they stood there, staring into each other's eyes and hoping to air more of their heartfelt love, Heaven leaned closer and kissed Jazz like she had never done before. They shared the beautiful taste of each other's lips as though it would be the last time. The ladies broke apart only when they heard a hearty laugh coming from the decorated wagon, where Hilly had been witnessing the wedding the entire day. Heaven turned to look at her baby. "I chose life, and I choose to live because of you two. I will never be selfish or put myself in harm's way ever again."

Jazz planted a warm kiss on Hilly's head and smiled. "How are you enjoying Bora Bora?" The weather was wonderful, the skies were clear, and the refreshing air coursing through their lungs continued to grant them the warmest feelings they could have ever imagined. "What next?" Jazz asked. "Now that you're legally and officially mine, what happens next?" Heaven handed her daughter to Jazz before leaning over to pick up the urn she wanted to be with them during their wedding on the beach in Bora Bora. Dragging her pretty wedding dress through the sand, she carried the urn around and slowly began to release her mother's ashes into the beach. "I am sorry Mommy you couldn't actually witness everything." Heaven sighed. "I really miss you, and I cannot thank you enough for your love and continuous kindness even when I was being a shitty child." Her eyes welled up with tears, and she couldn't keep them for long.

They rolled down one at a time, and soon a flood of teardrops washed down her cheeks before Jazz and Hilly joined her in staring at the beach. "She would have loved to have been here," Jazz assured Heaven. Heaven sniffed and with a somber tone, replied, "I miss her so much." They shared the moment in silence, except when Hilly interrupted with cackles and laughter. It was Heaven's happiest and saddest day at the same time.

She would have loved her mother to be there when she said those words of confirmation to Jazz. "I will always love you Mommy," Heaven whispered. Jazz simply nodded her head and answered, "I know you will, and I will always do the same as well."

A week later on Monday

A week had passed since their solo wedding, and Heaven could not believe what she was on the verge of doing. Looking back at how far she had come and how fast her business was growing, not just in size but popularity, and the amount it was bringing in monthly, she figured the need to bring an end to a rather disturbing episode was near at heart.

Knowing the love of her life and newly wedded partner was in the car with their baby girl waiting for her, Heaven walked through the doors of her office with the biggest smile on her face as people smiled and waved at her with some words of congratulations.

It had definitely taken some time for her to return, and it indeed was time for her to close out this chapter in life with the federal government.

She walked past the whiteboard and smiled, seeing her name had been enlisted under some really tough tasks. Her supervisor, no doubt, was at it again—jealous, hating, and above all, being petty as always. "When is she ever going to learn?" Heaven asked herself. It was the question on her lips as she approached the woman's office without an ounce of fear, or any measure of worry in her gut, either. Armed with the most important paper with which she was going to get her freedom from an institution she felt was restricting her from honing her creative skills, Heaven knocked on the door with the name "Margaret Rhode" embedded into it, and waited. "Come in," the voice commanded.

Heaven walked through the door with a spring in her step and a smug expression on her face.

Considering how well her business was doing, she was certain Margaret would have heard about it already.

"Look what the cat dragged in," the woman said with some disdain in her tone. She lacked compassion for what Heaven had experienced and why she had been on extended leave.

"Waltzing into my office on your first day back when you ought to resume work, your desk is piled high, deadlines are looming, my God what do you want, more work?"

Heaven retorted immediately. "Well, I was thinking it is time I step away from your bitterness and allow myself to grow, which is what every woman should do when they work under people or persons like you." She slammed the resignation letter in her hand on top of the table and watched the dumbfounded woman, who was unsure of how best to respond. Heaven had won, and she knew it. Slowly, she walked out of the office knowing she was the bigger person, and that there was absolutely nothing Margaret could do to hurt her, ever. She returned to the other offices where her resignation letter had to pass through, and within half an hour, Heaven felt herself become unburdened and unshackled by the problems of the other women. While she made her exit through the door, people stood on either side of the hallway to give her a round of applause in what looked like a guard of honor.

"You are really doing well," someone said.

"You have given a lot of us the inspiration to do better even when the world is crazy!" another said.

She couldn't quite understand what they were going on about, but it did make her emotional as she returned to her car to see Jazz and her baby.

"The most interesting thing happened after I dropped my resignation letter," she later said to Jazz.

Jazz chuckled and seemed unfazed by the occurrence.

"You are a superstar now. Haven't you seen the waves Glamour Girls Travel is making?" Jazz reminded her before starting the car and driving her family home.

Heaven sighed in relief, smiled at herself and the progress she was making so far, before finally agreeing to the fact that she was indeed on the rise and at a tremendous rate too.

Heaven wasn't sure how to tell Jazz their lives were about to change in a really crazy manner, but she was sure hiding it wasn't something she could even do. Their home had been blessed beyond measure, and blessing after blessing continued to fall into place in ways she couldn't quite imagine. She glanced at the offer being made before her as though it was impossible but knew there was just no messing around when it came to the people standing before her. It was her fifth meeting within a week and seemed like it was about to be the last and the one to seal the deal. The representatives from WalDart stood with an offer of no less than one and half million dollars to sign her up as their official distributor and provider of her famed Glamour Girls beach towels. Heaven's hand shuddered as she attempted to sign on the dotted lines meant to seal the deal.

Her lawyer had gone through the documents and promised everything was in order. She slowly tailed her signature across the lines, got up, and headed out of the building without being sure of what had just happened.

The amount of money and the deal, which could span into more contracts, rang in her head.

"Fuck! Fuck! Fuck!" she cried before getting into her car. She had just signed one of the biggest deals of her life.

It was a deal of a lifetime, and she could not believe that WalDart had chosen her to be their official supplier. She sped back home, unsure of how many traffic laws she had violated and how much trouble she could get herself into.

"Babe! Babe!" she cried out for Jazz the moment she walked through the door. Heaven's face froze as she stood and stared at Breezy standing in her living room.

He definitely wasn't welcome in there without prior notice, and Heaven slowly took her spot beside Jazz who motioned for her to come over.

"He has something to tell you, honey." Jazz spoke in such cool and relaxing tone that Heaven didn't quite know what to say.

"I needed to give this to you in person," he said, stretching out his hand with a note in it. "Read it after I leave, please." It felt odd, surreal, and really bothersome as they watched him head out of the room. The moment he stepped out, Heaven tore through the note, wondering what sour news he had brought her again. "This bastard had better not be suing me for custody of my baby or else I will…" She paused and felt her eyes catch on some rather pleasing words.

"Dear Heaven,

I know we aren't in the best of places in the moment and I know nothing I say or do can ever make amends for the turmoil I caused you through my nonchalant nature, lack of drive and the despicable act of getting your best friend pregnant. I am also sorry for the loss of your mother. I know how special she was and meant to you. I have made one bad mistake after another since we have been together except one, which is Hilly.

In an effort to make one additional good thing out of this, I reached out to my other uncle, the Chairman of WalDart, regarding finding a way to help secure our daughter's life and ensuring she never has to go through what either of us did over the past few years. He agreed to sign a contract with you on behalf of Hilly and a binding one, which ensures life will be fully secured for you two as long as you live.

I am sorry for everything once again and I wish you and Jazz a happy life.

Breezy"

"Oh my God!" Heaven screamed.

Breezy was behind the WalDart deal. Breezy's other uncle is one of the owners of the largest retail chains in the United States, WalDart.

She crumpled to her knees and wept in joy. Jazz hugged her warmly while Heaven's phone began to buzz with messages.

"Baby," Jazz called out to her, "you have some top magazines in the country asking to interview you." After the deal was signed, WalDart immediately released a press release "From Section 8 To C.E.O, The Inspiring Story of Heather Davis". Heaven turned to look at the television, shocked and surprised as information of the proposed deal was being aired on different television stations.

"These people mean business," Jazz muttered. Heaven didn't expect anything less from them, and she made up her mind not to disappoint as well.

"Did Breezy mention anything about talk shows?" Jazz asked.

Heaven shook her head and took the phone from her partner to read some of the invitations to share her life story on live television with people.

This deal had brought Heaven more exposure than she could have ever imagined in her lifetime. "I need to get myself a good team," Heaven noted. Heaven experienced a come-up in both status and prestige, and she needed a capable team to manage the helm of affairs for her. "We should start recruiting for the best staff ever, then," Jazz said. The two ladies got right to work.

A year had passed since Heaven got the two most important deals of her life (WalDart and the airline) and more kept coming through.

She and Jazz sat in the back of their limousine, awaiting the chauffeur to assist with the door. In that moment, everything went blank, and she allowed her mind to roam through events from the past. "I would have never assumed I would be here today." It was what made telling her tale of driving and grinding hard from Section 8 to becoming a CEO of a multimillion-dollar corporation so interesting. It was even more wonderful having Jazz by her side. Jazz smiled and yawned a bit before stretching. "I don't know how you do it, but these public appearances are really draining. But I love them and I love you, so I don't care."

Ever since their press conference with the *New York Times*, *Fashion Gxd Magazine*, *Urban Magazine*, *Essence* magazine, *Ebony* magazine, *Black Enterprise,* and *People* magazine, the events just wouldn't end. It was safe to say going into a deal with Breezy's uncle opened the doors into public life more than they ever could have imagined. "I have something to tell you before we head out there tonight," Jazz said with an emotional expression on her face.

"What is it?" Heaven asked in a concerned tone as people had begun to cheer for them outside their vehicle.

Jazz had kept the news to herself for the past few days, waiting for the perfect moment to air it.

"I got added to the roster for the Washington Mystics women's basketball team!!!" Jazz said.

"This means my time with you might be limited when we start to go on the road for games." Heaven's face dropped in tempo, but she soon donned a smile. "You forget I'm a successful woman now and seeing you whenever I want isn't going to be a problem." She giggled. "Nothing is ever going to keep me away from you." Jazz had expected nothing less as they embraced and shared a passionate kiss.

"Your fans are waiting." Jazz pulled away and pointed at the window. Heaven pulled her back, kissed her once again, and replied, "Our fans, you mean?"

The two stepped out of the car to raucous applause and whistles. It was what they were showered with on every television show they got invited to, and Heaven couldn't help but soak in the adoration every single time. Jazz seemed to fancy it too, as the duo waved at their fans and blew them kisses before heading into the building, where one of the most remarkable and respected television hosts was waiting for them. She was about to speak to women regarding the DC Housing Program, hoping to inspire and motivate them about a woman of color who had to push hard against the odds to become who she was in that moment as a CEO, starting from a Section 8 beneficiary.

It was just one more avenue, like the others when she traveled the states with Jazz, to educate people on life in general as a lesbian, a mother, a businesswoman, and a survivor in a world so dominated by hate, disappointments, and men. "I have something special in my heart which I have been planning to share with you," Heaven whispered to Jazz as they got on stage.

"What is it?" Jazz asked excitedly. Heaven placed a finger to her lips and replied, "Don't ruin the surprise, darling." Two days later, they launched a foundation in support and remembrance of Heaven's mother. Heaven promised herself that losing her mother would serve as a catalyst to educate and empower families of stroke survivors. She named the foundation Surviving After Losing A Loved One to a Stroke. She could only wonder what her mother must be thinking of her from above. Heaven was sure her mom would be proud, and it was all she could ever ask for. With tears in her eyes as she remembered her dear mother, she waved at the cameras, knowing thousands and hundreds of thousands of other women like herself were watching and listening to learn and hear what she had to say.

Heaven cleared her throat, took in subtle breaths, and with the permission of the television host, began her story as a woman who had moved from Section 8 to become the CEO seated before them. Her life would become an inspiration for others in ways even she might never come to imagine. Yet, it was Heaven's way of giving back. She had seen it all, and she remained standing as the survivor she was and the victorious woman she had shaped herself to be. Armed with the presence of the most important woman in her life, Heaven was sure everything she had just achieved was the starting point not just for her, but also for her family as a whole.

About Kinyatta E. Gray

Kinyatta E. Gray is a Best-Selling Author, Celebrity Travel Influencer and CEO of FlightsInStilettos. Kinyatta wrote and released her first book in 2019, a memoir, *30 Days: Surviving the Trauma and Unexpected Loss of a Single Parent as an Only Child*. Kinyatta's aspirations to become an author were as a result of a heart-gripping moment in her mom's final moments of life. She committed to honoring her mother's legacy by becoming a published author. Kinyatta's mother wanted to be a published author but passed away in 2018 before ever realizing her dream. Kinyatta has acquired the support of the biggest talent in the entertainment industry to support her books. The celebrities who have conveyed support for *30 Days*, the memoir, are: Yandy Smith CEO of *EGL Magazine* and TV personality; TV personality Antoine Von Boozier; MaMa Kim from VH1 Love & Hip-Hop NYC; Florina Kaja from Oxygen's *The Bad Girls Club*; rapper Soo Vegaz, CEO of New Jersey's largest radio station Time2 Grind; Madison Jaye, Celebrity Podcaster, iHeartRadio, Pilar Scratch, Celebrity Public Relations Expert, Always Ask Asia, Radio One Personality; and celebrity wardrobe stylist Jasmine Hill-Carter. Rising in success, Kinyatta has been featured in a variety of press outlets: iHeartRadio and Pandora *The Madison Jaye Show*, *Fashion Gxd Magazine*, *Medium*, *Vine Magazine*, *The Bunnie Hole*, *Mogul*, *My Girl Gang*, *The Culture Report*, *The Davi Magazine*, *Authority Magazine*, *Thrive Global*, *Pen Legacy*, *Daily Inside Scoop*, *Billionaire Magazine*, *IMU Media*, *Definitely Amazing*, *Urban Magazine*, and *The LA Cocina Podcast*, just to name a few.

Kinyatta's memoir was a sponsor of the Christmas event for Carol Maraj, the mother of hip-hop icon Nikki Minaj.

Website: KinyattaGray.com
Website: FlightsInStilettos.com
Instagram: @kinyattagraytheauthor & @flightsinstilettos
Facebook: KinyattaGraytheauthor & MrsKinyatta

How many times have you felt invisible in a room full of people? How many masks have you worn to hide your true identity? How many heterosexual relationships did you engage in pretending to be in love? What was your biggest fear when finally letting your family and friends know, you are a beautiful feminine lesbian?

Passing As "Straight": Beautiful Women Whose True Sexuality Went Undetected by a Judgmental Society, compiled by Author Kinyatta Gray, brings to life a book that takes a deep look into the individual, personal and complex stories of lesbians whose true sexuality went undetected to prevent labeling, judgment, or even death. Six courageous women will share real life situations where they had to make the dreadful decision of hiding their sexual identify to find acceptance, respect, and love from those who truly matter.

This book is not meant to define who's right or wrong, but rather examine this very real issue and the choices that lesbian women must make about love! Our intention is to provide a heartfelt resource for women who wake up daily having to navigate through a society pretending and hiding who they really are. You are not alone! We all have been there! But, as you read through these pages, you will find the comfort and strength to know exactly how to live unapologetically and uniquely who you are.

KINYATTA E. GRAY, CELEBRITY AUTHOR
INSTAGRAM: @KINYATTAGRAYTHEAUTHOR
WEBSITE: KINYATTAGRAY.COM

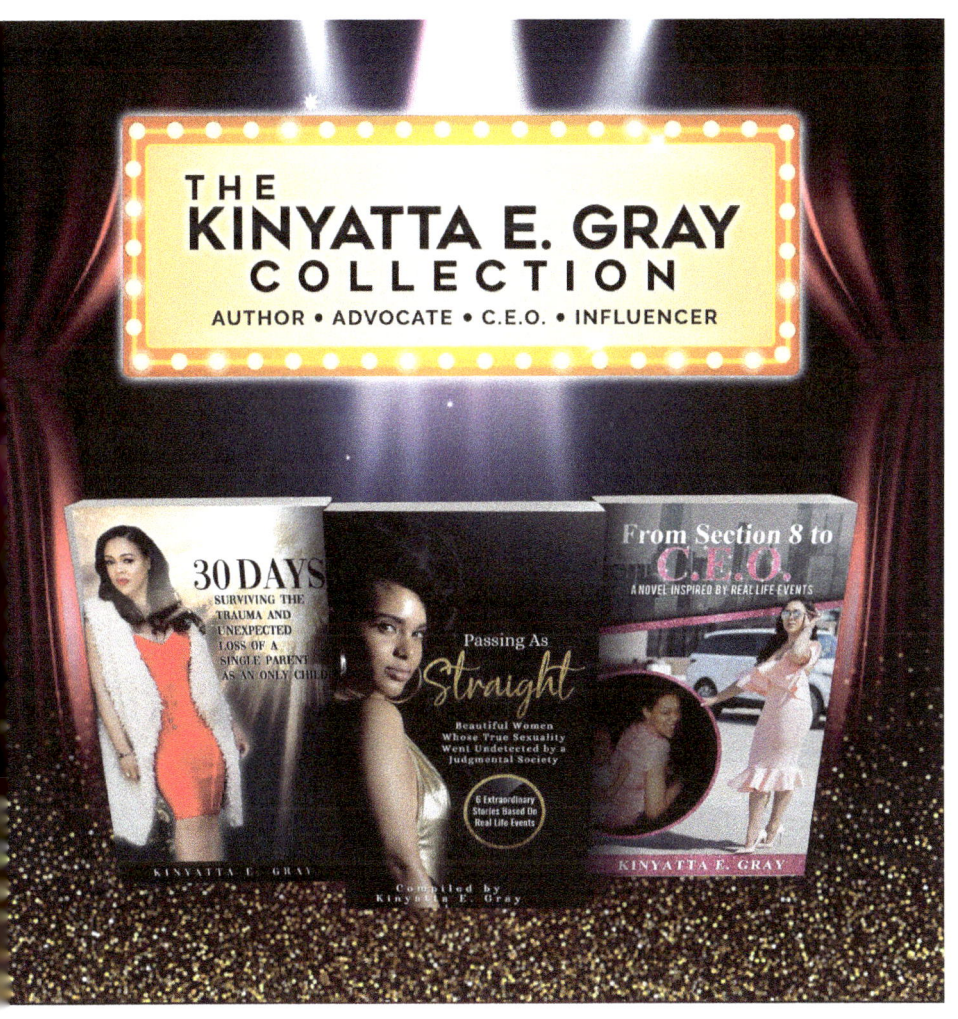

THE MADISON JAYE SHOW ON
ANDORA
iHeart
"I had to dig
in deep for my
healing because
i knew my
mother would
never leave me,
she was now my
guardian
angel."
KINYATTA E
GRAY AUTHOR, CELEBRITY
TRAVEL INFLUENCER,
CREATOR

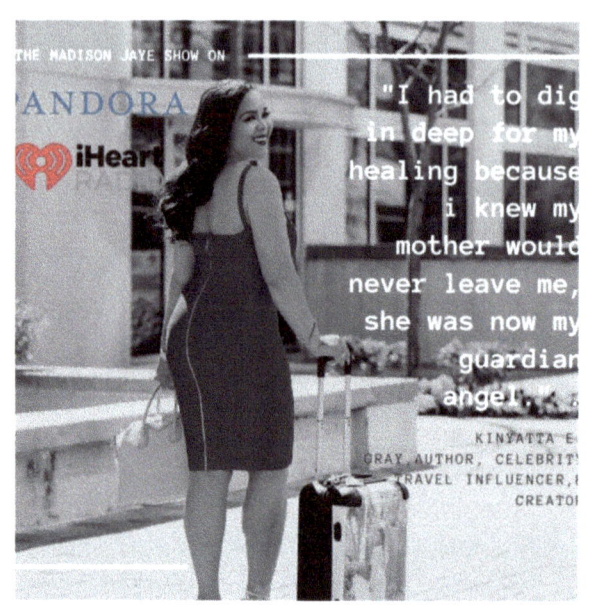

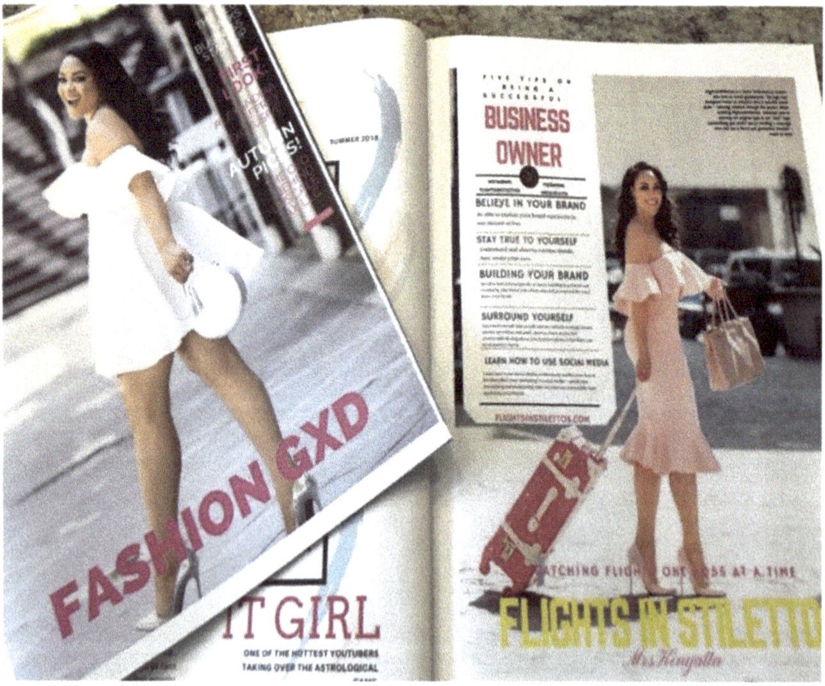

FASHION GXD
SUMMER 2018
IT GIRL
ONE OF THE HOTTEST YOUTUBERS
TAKING OVER THE ASTROLOGICAL
BUSINESS
OWNER
BELIEVE IN YOUR BRAND
STAY TRUE TO YOURSELF
BUILDING YOUR BRAND
SURROUND YOURSELF
LEARN HOW TO USE SOCIAL MEDIA
FLIGHTS IN STILETTO
Mrs Kinyatta

Kinyatta E. Gray Magazine Feature

Kinyatta E. Gray's Appearance on *BMORE Lifestyle* on MyTV Baltimore

www.ingramcontent.com/pod-product-compliance
Lightning Source LLC
Chambersburg PA
CBHW042113100526
44587CB00025B/4037